Let My People Go!

A Modern Day Exodus for Every Bound Up Believer

By Lisa Clements

May you hear
a *personal* word
from the Lord
as you read.

Lisa :)

2 COR 9:8

Contents

A note from the author

⸺⊙⸺

The Bible says "He chose the simple things to confound the wise." I don't know if I qualify as confounding anyone, but I do qualify as simple. I am not a theologian nor do I pastor a church. I am a Bible teacher by gifting and I have a passion for the Word of God. I have not lived my life perfectly, in fact most of my experiences come from the myriad of mistakes I have made, but it is in those places that I have come to know God, His amazing grace, His forgiving heart, His merciful ways and His unconditional love. My family is not perfect either. We do not qualify as "the Cleavers." We look more like "the Clampitts", but we are a work in progress and our hope is in God, knowing that the work He began in each one of us He will complete. So it is not out of perfection, nor training, nor degrees or titles that this book comes forth. It comes forth by "a call" from God to take pen in hand and to write for Him. I had no aspiration to write a book. In fact "the call" to do so nearly unglued me! It has taken a prayer team of over fifty people just to keep me from being anxious about such a God sized task, to keep me focused on God and not the lack of my abilities, and to keep me in the quiet place to hear His voice.

When the Lord spoke this book into being He did so because He said His church was in bondage and He wants us free. I asked the Lord why the church is in bondage. He gave me two reasons. He said, "They don't know truth or they don't apply truth." It became apparent early in the writing of this book, that these would be the two areas He desired to speak to— *knowing truth and applying truth.*

I have had a front row seat to watch this book unfold. I have been awed by the heart of God. There is much in this book I would have never included if left up to me because…well, because I am human and often desire to take the "less painful" route. Sometimes "truth" hurts, but more often than not it is the surgery for the soul – a very necessary and needed operation. It is such "cutting" truth the Lord has chosen to pen in this book. He says it best in His own words, **"You shall know the truth and the truth shall set you free**." God wants His church free and the route to freedom begins with truth – *knowing and applying.* I am grateful to God for the many truths I have learned in this journey of the book. I will never be the same again. I hope as you read that you, too, will be transformed by these truths and the loving heart of God for you.

Lisa Clements

Acknowledgements

I always wait on the key grips! My husband has long since given up on getting me to leave the movies before they show the key grips. When the credits roll, their names are not the first, not even in the middle, but most always last. Most people never know who the key grips are or even what they do. But I've always imagined a proud parent somewhere, enduring the endless list of names, for that one name they came to see, their kid, the key grip. They didn't produce or direct the movie. They weren't in charge of costumes or make-up. No, their jobs were much more subtle, a behind the scenes kind of thing, but vital nonetheless.

I have a lot of "key grips" I want to give credit to. They didn't write the book, or publish it, or even illustrate, but they encouraged me, prayed for me, inspired me and spurred me on. They are people, real people who have participated in what God desired and destined in the writing of this book. I ask you to remain seated, to not leave, as I let the credits role. More than a thank you goes to:

Melanie Matthews and Jen Palmer - for being willing messengers for God. This was huge confirmation! Thanks you for being bold and speaking.
My Prayer Team – my heart is grateful more than I could ever express. God will remember your work in the Prayer Closet and reward you.
Pastor Don Thrasher – your encouragement and Godly advice was

invaluable. Thank you for being there when the spiritual warfare was heavy.

Debbie Ferguson - your load has been great. As my accountability partner you have had to bear much, however, you love so easily and encourage so wonderfully, it has blessed me beyond measure.

Debbie Currie – you are wise beyond your years. Your counsel is solid and your discernment on target. I am deeply indebted and blessed.

Elizabeth Taylor - my "God-friend", you picked me up time and time again. Your spiritual CPR has revived me more times than I can count. My heart is thankful.

My Proofreaders, Robin Dill, Melanie Matthews, Bridget Clark and Pastor Don - God said He would provide and He did! Your job was large!

My family – each of you have such a special place in my heart. To my children *Jenny, Colby,* and *Candace* I say thank you for the joy you give me on a daily basis. I love you so much it hurts. Jenny, your typing of the manuscript was a gift from heaven.

To my Parents and my Sisters – oh my goodness –could we write a book on our adventures? I have learned much from you and by being family. Through thick and thin God has sustained us on this wild ride called life. Thank you for being long-suffering with me.

To my husband Tim – Thank you for being so willing to do whatever was necessary for this book to come forth. The day I shared the vision of this book, the tears in your eyes when you said, "I know this is God" was all I needed to go forward. I love you and I am grateful to God for giving you to me.

Lisa

Introduction

It was a 1956 blockbuster that hit the silver screen with all the fan fair of *Gone with the Wind*. The preview party was set and the Hollywood elite showed up to view the epic that would become a classic. With a movie cast of thousands, filmed on location in Egypt and the region of Sinai, the release of Cecil B. DeMille's *The Ten Commandments*, had long been awaited. The spotlight appeared, the kettle drums rolled, the curtains parted and out walked Mr. DeMille. He spoke gently and with conviction as he shared with his audience the impetus behind the making of such a movie. He said simply, *"This may seem an unusual procedure speaking to you before the picture begins, but we have an unusual subject, the story of the birth of freedom."* He continued, *"Our intent was not to create a story but to be worthy of the divinely inspired story created 3,000 years ago."* And with that said the lights dimmed, the overture began and the large curtains pulled back. A simple message appeared on the big screen, *"Those who see this motion picture will make a pilgrimage over the very ground that Moses trod more than 3,000 years ago.[1]"* The message disappeared and the movie began.

Perhaps that message was larger and louder than the movie itself. While Mr. DeMille may have been talking subjectively, I believe it is a spiritual truism of a journey all God's people must take. Everybody has an Egypt – a place in our lives where we have felt bound, unable to escape ourselves, our sins, or even our adversary. It's a place we don't want to be and yet we are there and it seems we are unable to leave. Our Egypt is often strewn with broken dreams, plans that went awry, unwise decisions, weak lifestyles, and the list goes on. Disappointment abounds often in ourselves and others. For us, it's a different day, but the same story of bondage and slavery.

If history repeats, and it does, then there is hope for us in the story of the birth of freedom; hope that God still hears, hope that God still delivers and hope that God still sets people free. Such a story of truth and triumph intrigues the Cecil B. DeMille in all of us. It's a story worthy of recalling because it reveals a passage way to the Promise Land in every one of our lives. The road out of Egypt is as old as the book of Exodus itself. It's time tested and has been traveled by generation after generation. You are not the first nor will you be the last to walk such a route of freedom. The important thing right now is that every child of God knows that when God told Moses to say **"Let my people go!"** He meant it! He speaks to the Pharaoh's of our lives and commands the same release. Know this: when God speaks, things happen! God says in Isaiah 55:10-11,

As the rain and the snow come down from heaven, and do not return to it without watering the earth and making it bud and flourish, so that it yields seed for the sower and bread for the eater, so is my word that goes out from my mouth: It will not return to me empty, but will accomplish what I desire and achieve the purposed for which I sent it.

Some 3,000 years ago, God spoke these words of freedom, "Let my people go." The words will not return back to God until they have accomplished His expressed purpose generation after generation after generation. Egypt is a crowded place, look around, you are not alone. Not everyone is bound by the same circumstance, situation, relationship, habit, lifestyle, addiction, thoughts or demons. But everyone gets to Egypt by the same wrong turn.

Its route is disguised and yet it is well known. It's the road of rebellion, the highway of hard-headedness and the interstate of imitation, worldly imitation. Make no mistake; all such roads lead to Egypt. We often wonder how to get out, but never wonder how we got in. Most all know the day they took the wrong turn. Egypt's lure is the land of the gods, gods known only as personal wealth, influence, power, lust, desires, or pleasure. Such gods sing like sirens on the coastal highways of our lives, seducing us to a lesser life through a simple song of deceit. Ears not *trained in truth* will succumb to such a song that makes even the seemingly strongest among us abandon the boat of blessing for the land of lack. Those camped out in Egypt sooner or later find out all that glitters is not gold, the grass on the other side is not always greener, a greedy man's stomach is never filled, and a plan apart from God never prevails. The Bible says, **"There is a way that *seems* right to man but therein leads to death."** (Proverbs 14:12; emphasis mine) Such death could be emotional, mental, relational, or even physical.

Egypt is an entrapment of the soul through the weakness of the man – little portals in our lives where sin, self, or Satan seeks to grab hold of, takes a strong hold of, the control panel of our destiny. These "reckless drivers" sooner or later illicit a cry from even the bravest passengers on board, a cry from the soul that captures the ears of our Father. Make no doubt about it, heaven hears and heaven responds to such a cry.

The Lord said, "I have indeed seen the misery of my people in Egypt. *I have heard* them crying out because of their slave drivers and I am concerned about their suffering. So I have come down to rescue them…and to bring them up out of that land into a good and spacious land flowing with milk and honey" (Exodus 3:7-8; emphasis mine).

God has a rescue plan for every one of His children. It was set in place before the beginning of time. It's a plan that frees the oppressed, the weak, the confused, the strong, the successful, the miserable, the independent, and the co-dependent, the lost, the found, the grieved, the happy, the sad, the lonely, and the one who cries and the one who can't cry, any and all who are trapped in Egypt.

God knows the "route to freedom" and stands today as a neon sign saying, "This way." For all who seek, they shall find. God said to Moses, **"Tell Pharaoh to let my people go."** The road to freedom has been cut and cleared. The release has been declared for God's people, *all* God's people.

Whether you turn to the right to the left your ears will hear a voice behind you saying, "This is the way; walk in it." (Isaiah 30:21)

Realization of such freedom is the on ramp to the Promised Land. One needs only to receive such realization, such revelation by faith. Walking the route of freedom is a *faith walk* and *requires daily direction* from the One who knows the way. While there may be many roads that lead to Egypt, only *one* leads out. Such a road to freedom begins at that identifiable place in our lives where we realize that "apart from Him we can do nothing.

Stand at the crossroads and ask for the ancient paths, ask where the good way is and walk in it and you will find rest for you souls. (Jeremiah 6:16)

It begins when we believe the Word of God, receive the Word of God, and begin by faith to walk out the Word of God. Aha! The route to freedom revealed; an ancient path still available for all whom desire to leave. The exit sign is marked "surrender", the on ramp, "revelation", the highway is the "way of truth", and the destination is the "Promised Land". The Promised Land... the place of God's presence, provision and power— the resting place of our souls. If you are ready to receive such a roadmap to freedom then turn the page and let's get started.

I ask that the God of our Lord Jesus Christ, the Glorious Father, may give you a *spirit of wisdom and revelation*, so that you may know Him better. I pray also that the *eyes of your heart may be enlightened* in order that you may know the hope to which He has called you, the riches of His glorious inheritance in the saints, and His incomparable great power for us who believe. (Ephesians 1:17-19a; emphasis mine)

Chapter 1

The Story of the Birth of Freedom

"Let My People Go!"

Let us take a good look at the way we are living
and re-order our lives under God.

(Lamentations 3:40; *The Message*)

The Story of the Birth of Freedom

The story of the birth of freedom is as old as the book of Exodus and as time tested as the Bible itself. I can relay to you the story because I have traveled the route to freedom personally and have learned of the route by revelation through God's Word. It's a route that never changes and is available for every believer who so desires to travel such a way.

The story begins in Exodus at a most unusual place, the sight of a burning bush. You probably know this part of the story. God calls out to Moses from the burning bush and reveals to Moses something He has heard. Moses removes his sandals and stands on the burning sand in front of a burning bush and listens as God speaks. In the quietness and surrealness of that moment, God imparts to Moses the "hearings" of His heart.

The Lord said, "I have indeed seen the misery of my people in Egypt. I have *heard* them crying out because of their slave drivers and I am concerned about their suffering. So I have come down to rescue them from the hand of the Egyptians and to bring them up out of that land into a good and spacious land flowing with milk and honey..." (Exodus 7 – 8a; emphasis mine).

The Lord reveals to Moses that He is well aware of the suffering and enslavement of His people. He has heard their cries; the loud wailing and the muted whimpering of hearts too broken to have volume. He has seen their misery and knows even the source of their agony, anguish, and calamity. He knows the sources by name and categorizes them only as "slave drivers." He tells Moses that He has come down and is present for a purpose. The purpose is that of freedom. It's rescue 9-1-1 and God is on the scene. His plan includes the movement of His people from the place of captivity and confinement to the land of liberty and love. It's spacious, He says, giving hint that numbers are no problem and provisions for many has been made. Then out of the bush God suddenly reveals page two of Plan One when He speaks personally to Moses these words:

"So now go; I am sending you to Pharaoh to bring my people the Israelites out of Egypt" (Exodus 3:10).

And Moses does what any of us would do; he starts to stutter and offers up his first words of debate and excuse to such a mission.

"Who am I, that I should go to Pharaoh and bring the Israelites out of Egypt?" (Exodus 3:11)

God bypasses the question and discloses more of his plan.

"I will be with you. And this will be the sign to you that it is I who have sent you; when you have brought the people out of Egypt, you will worship God on this mountain" (Exodus 3:12).

Retain the last part of that scripture, we'll talk about it later, but for now Moses doesn't sign on so easily. He's got questions, big questions.

"Suppose I go (remember I'm not committed yet!) to the Israelites and say to them, 'The God of your fathers has sent me to you, and they ask me, 'What is His Name?' Then what shall I tell them?" (Exodus 3:13; emphasis mine).

Good question from Moses. A good question because up until this time Moses has only known of God through others, mainly his wife and his father-in-law Jethro. Though Moses was born a Hebrew, he was a raised an Egyptian and only knew God second hand. He stepped into his heritage some would say by accident, others by divine orchestration. Nevertheless, today was Moses' day to come to know God personally. It was a meeting in the desert and it had been on God's calendar for years! It was here in this moment God revealed His identity to Moses for all mankind to hear. The question hung in the air "What is his name?" "What shall I tell them?" Moses waited. Out of the burning bush the Rock of Ages, the Master of Heaven, the Architect and Builder of the World, the Creator of Heaven and Earth, the Consuming fire, the Most High God, the Maker of All Things, the Helper, the Hiding Place, the Comforter and Confidant, The Mighty One, the Righteous Father answers. The trees stood still, the breeze came to a halt, the birds stopped fluttering and the clouds hovered. All creation paid attention as the voice of all time spoke.

"'I AM WHO I AM'. This is what you are to say to the Israelites. 'I AM' has sent me to you. This is my name forever, the name by which I am to be remembered from generation to generation" (Exodus 3:14, 15b).

Out of the burning bush God told Moses how He signs His checks. The personal name of God as it is written on His account. "I AM." The name speaks volumes. It was as if God was giving Himself a nickname. "I AM" was short for:

I AM the Alpha and Omega, the beginning and the end.
I AM the Bread of Life.
I AM the Light of the World.
I AM the Gate and the Good Shepherd.
I AM the Resurrection and the Life.
I AM the Living Water.
I AM the True Vine.
I AM the Lord who heals, the Lord who provides.

I AM the Word of Life, the Wonderful Counselor, the Deliverer and Redeemer.
I AM the Way, the Truth, and the Life.
I AM the King of Kings and the Lord of Lords.
I AM.

The revelation of who God is, is so encompassing, so profound, and so immense, that this day in the desert, the realness of God shortened His name to I AM. It would be the name that Moses would carry to the people, the name that would open prison doors and set captives free, the name that would bind up the broken hearted and proclaim the release for every prisoner.

Moses heard the answer but had other questions, **"What if they do not believe me or listen to me and say, 'The Lord did not appear to you?' "** Moses needed validation of the message and the mission God was about to send him on. We all do! And God was about to give it. He told Moses to throw down his staff. Moses threw it on the ground and it became a snake. God told him to reach and take the snake by the tail and it turned back into a staff. God told Moses to put his hand inside his coat. He did. When he took it out it "was leprous like snow." In returning his hand to his coat, it was restored "like the rest of his flesh." God was allowing Moses to experience the nature of who He is. The supernatural God, the God of the miraculous, the God of signs, wonders, and miracles. All of which would accompany Moses on his mission in Egypt. As the story unfolded Moses reached his destination among the captives and told them everything the great "I AM" has said.

He performed the signs before the people of God and they believed. And when they heard that the Lord was concerned about them and had seen their misery they bowed down and worshipped (Exodus 4:30-31).

Push pause for a moment. Linger right here. Come with me to a higher place, a vantage point and let's have a look - a long look – a panoramic look of the first impact of the message. It's a heart breaking sight. Blistered, bruised, and broken bodies bowed everywhere.

Days of doubt, months of murmuring, and years of yokes have brought the captives to their knees when the "deliverer" arrives on the scene. Could this be real? Could this true? The Bible simply says, "They believed." What about you? God has made no less provision for His people today. Moses was a type and picture of the One who was coming to be the Deliverer for all mankind. His name is Jesus and God sent Him so that **"none should perish but have eternal life" (John 3:16).** Jesus is our Deliverer, the One who comes with truth, the Good News of the release that God has declared. He is the Lamp unto our feet and the Light unto path. He is the narrow way, the only way, and He stands at the exit door of Egypt saying, "Follow me." He is the anointed One who can indeed set captives free. He is the one who can break the bonds of evil and proclaim freedom from sin and satanic oppression. He alone opens spiritual eyes and spiritual doors that all may go through— all that is, that so desire.

So the question remains, "What about you?" Do you believe? The Israelites believed by faith in the words God sent them through Moses. *Believing* is the first step of freedom for everyone, even you. Believing is an action of the heart not the lips. To believe means: to adhere to, to rely on, and trust in.[1] Moses did not speak words of his own, but carried the message of God to the people. They had a choice to believe or not to believe. They had a choice to adhere to, rely on and trust in God or... not. He was either the way out of their bondage or He wasn't. They had to make a decision. So do you.

Pharaoh's Release

Afterward Moses and Aaron went to Pharaoh and said, "This is what the Lord the God of Israel says, 'Let my people go, that they may worship me in the desert.' "Pharaoh said, 'Who is this Lord that I should obey him and let Israel go? I do not know the Lord and I will not let Israel go' " (Exodus 5:1-2).

Moses boldly spoke the word God gave him to the king of captivity, the Pharaoh. Pharaoh didn't care; he didn't even seem to budge. The declaration and demand was like a fruit fly, a little nuisance of the moment. He issued his response, **"I will not let Israel go"** **(Exodus 5:2).**

Know this— bondage can speak! It does have a voice and a very strong will. This spirit of evil in the biblical sense will not lie down and play dead while you walk out. It will fight you with tenacity because it has an evil agenda and a power that feeds it. Devouring God's people is table food for Satan. He seeks to steal, to kill, and to destroy the purpose, the nature, the destiny of people. But Jesus, our Deliverer has arrived upon the scene **"that we may have life and have it to the fullest."**[1] He offers salvation, the way "out of Egypt" for all who will follow. The word "salvation" in Greek text means "deliverance," "bringing safely through," or "keeping from harm."[2] Our "saving One," our "Deliverer" is Jesus.

Acts 4:12 says, "Salvation is found in no one else, for there is no other name under heaven given to men by which we must be saved."

Moses was a foreshadow, a forerunner, and a foretaste, if you will, of the "One" who was to come. Moses was the messenger of the promise that would be fulfilled in Jesus Christ. The promise of freedom was from sin, Satan, and the world. He was sent as a minister of the message to Egypt, with a memo in hand for Pharaoh. It simply read, "Let my people go".... As the Israelites bowed down in surrender to the message and the One who sent it, life was about to change.

For Better or Worse?

That same day (the day Moses delivered the news to Pharaoh) Pharaoh gave this order to the slave drivers and foremen in charge of the people. "You are no longer to supply them with straw for making bricks; let them go and gather their own straw. But require them to make the same number of bricks as before; don't reduce the quota. They are lazy; that is why they are crying out, 'Let us go and sacrifice to our God.' Make the work harder for the men so that they keep working and pay no attention to lies" (Exodus 5:6-9; parenthesis mine).

The people had not anymore gotten up off their knees in hope until a cloud of doom settled in like a pyramid of bricks. Their hope seemed to turn to despair and the furnace of oppression was kicked up a notch! Just when they believed freedom was on the horizon, the demands of their slavery became vocally and physically stronger. After all, it was their own weakness that got them into Egypt. How would they ever overcome such powerful slave drivers?

Good question. Good question for us all. To find the answer we need only to look deeper into the story of the exodus – the exit – the way out for the people of God. The story line of the exodus is really about the conflict between two gods; the god of this world and the God of the universe. In the biblical time of Exodus, the Pharaoh in Egyptian religion was believed to be the incarnation of the sun god, *Re* [3]. Pharaoh was under the delusion that he was more powerful than the God of the Israelites. After all he had Israel enslaved. If their God was so powerful why were they bound? Hmmm. Let's go deeper. Israel didn't end up in Egypt by accident. They got there by choice, a choice made years earlier, that was born out of jealously and envy.

The nation of Israel was named for the father of the nation, a man named Israel. Israel's former name was Jacob. Jacob had twelve sons that became the twelve tribes of Israel or the Israelites. Israel's (Jacob's) favorite son was Joseph. Such favoritism of Joseph evoked a jealousy among the other brothers. Their jealously and envy led them to a plan to get rid of Joseph. The plan to get rid of a problem rather than deal with it has been around for a long time. The brothers schemed and eventually sold Joseph as a slave into the hands of Egyptians. Their bad behavior and actions opened the door to an enemy that would later put the entire nation of Israel into the same slavery. Years after selling Joseph a famine hit the land and the word of "grain in Egypt" reached Jacob and his sons. The aging father told his sons to make their way to Egypt to see if they could purchase some grain for their very existence. It was a much older and wiser Joseph, having been promoted through his faithfulness to God, who was now in charge of all the grain distribution of Egypt. Even though the brothers no longer recognized Joseph, Joseph recognized them. A picture of God's grace and mercy flowed forth from Joseph as he extended to them the same grace and love God had extended to him all those years away from family.

"Do not be distressed and do not be angry with yourselves for selling me here, because it was to save lives that God sent me ahead of you. God sent me a head of you to preserve for you a remnant on earth and to save your lives by a great deliverance" **(Genesis 45: 5-7).**

Joseph's message to his brothers was how God can overrule evil actions of humans in order to carry out His will. Genesis 50:21 captures Joseph's discourse with his brothers, **"You intended to harm me, but God intended it for good to accomplish what is now being done, the saving of many lives."** Romans 8:28 says it another way, **"And we know that God causes *all things* to work together for good for those who love God, to those who are called according to his purpose"** *(New American Standard).* One man's life (Joseph's) was given for many. Sound familiar? It was just the beginning of the unfolding of the story of freedom, the great deliverance. God had divinely allowed His people to settle in the land of Egypt, the birth bed of captivity and bondage. Jealousy and envy had opened the door of entrance. Famine escorted them in. It would be in Egypt that God's people would learn first hand of their need of a Savior and Deliverer; a way out of the imprisonment of their own sinful actions. The Israelites (Joseph's brothers at this point) were about to reap the consequence of such actions. But God was about to reveal that He can turn all things for good for those that love Him.

As the nation of Israel grew, the Egyptians became fearful that in sheer numbers alone, this nation might be able to overtake them. Such fear led a Pharaoh to oppress the people and take them as slaves for himself.

Now Joseph and all his brothers and all that generation died, but the Israelites were fruitful and multiplied greatly and became exceedingly numerous, so that the land was filled with them. Then a new king, who did not know about Joseph, came

to power in Egypt. 'Look,' he said to his people, 'the Israelites have become much too numerous for us. Come, we must deal shrewdly with them or they will become even more numerous and if war breaks out, will join our enemies fight against us and leave the country.' So they put slave masters over them to oppress them with forced labor.... They made their lives bitter with hard labor (Exodus 1:6-11a, 14).

The land of Egypt was never the desired destination of God for His people. But the divine plan of God allowed His people to experience consequences of bad behavior and bad decisions. God used the consequences to evoke a cry of the soul for freedom from the "slave masters" of such decisions. Such a cry sets into motion the plan of God. Such a cry causes God to intervene when the human soul gives way and surrenders in faith to God. It is the beginning of the birth of freedom for every man and woman. Moses, who was called by God, would be the minister who would carry the message, **"Let my people go."** The message was delivered to the people first and the slave masters second. The people had a choice to believe and receive the message of God or not. Their choice was **"and they believed"** (Exodus 4:31). The heart had been prepared. It was ready to be set free, awaiting such a word of freedom. It was sick of service to the slave master. And the question remains, "What about us?" Do we believe the message? Are we prepared to be set free?

"God has not deserted us in our bondage" (Ezra 9:9).
"Whom the Son sets free is free indeed" (John 8:36).
"God said, "Tell Pharaoh 'Let My people go' "(Exodus 7:16).

Chapter 2

Shake A Leg, You're Free!

Whom the Son sets free is free indeed.
(John 8:36)

Moses had questions and so do I. If God has provided freedom for "those who believe," then why are God's people (the modern day church) not free? It was precisely this question that I asked the Lord when He called me to write this book. In my heart, He responded with two reasons: He said, "They (the church) don't know truth or they don't apply truth." Immediately this scripture came into my heart, **"Whom the Son sets free is *free* indeed" (John 8:36; emphasis mine).**

Every blood bought redeemed child of God has freedom from sin and the slavery of sin and some don't even know it. Why? As the Lord said, "They don't know this truth or they are not applying this truth." This word from the Lord brought to mind a story I had heard a long time ago. It's the story of how elephants are trained.

Training Elephants

It is said that elephant trainers use chains around the feet of baby elephants to train them to not wander or run away. A baby elephant on the loose is one thing, a massive adult elephant meandering or on the rampage is quite another! Soon after birth, the baby elephant is chained and staked in one place. Disgruntled with the confinement, the small elephant will pull and tug at the chain, but can't get free. This may go on for a couple of years. However, somewhere in the course of training the elephant stops pulling. He knows he is chained and no longer puts up a resistance. The "pull" has gone out of him (so to speak). When the trainer recognizes this, it is then that the chains are actually removed. The habit of the elephant has been established. He no longer tries to get free because he "believes" he is chained. But the truth is the elephant is free! The elephant is free and he doesn't know it! He needs only to shake a leg and know that he is free!

This is such a picture of the church. Through the confession of and belief in Jesus Christ, we too are free!

We have freedom now, because Christ made us free. So stand strong. Do not change and go back to the slavery of the law (Galatians 5:1 New Century Version).

In Christ we are set free by the blood of his death and so we have forgiveness of sins (Ephesians 1:7 New Century Version).

But God set you free when he sent his own Son to be like us sinners and to be a sacrifice for our sin (Romans 8:3 New Century Version).

The day we bowed our heart before Jesus and sincerely asked Him to be Lord and Savior of our lives was the day we were set free. It's the day the chains of slavery to sin were removed. Up until this point we had been slaves, staked down to our own sinfulness. We couldn't move past it and had no ability to get free. But Jesus came into our lives by invitation and He set us free from our past, our present, and our future, hence, "Whom the Son sets free is free indeed."

So why is the church still acting as if it is bound? Why are God's people caught up in sinful actions, behavior and lifestyles? Why is the enemy of this world able to wreak such havoc on our lives? Two reasons:

Absence of truth (we don't know it!)

Absence of application of truth (we don't apply it!)

Knowing Truth

The truth is that before we come to salvation in Jesus Christ we are "slaves" to sin and sin's power. We have no power within us to overcome indefinitely the enormous temptations of sin. The expression "sold as a slave to sin" is a picture of us. We are in bondage to sin's power and cannot get free. It's what "Egypt" is all about. Egypt is a metaphor for the world. It's the place where sin, self and Satan rule. Egypt is a picture of the entrapment of this world. Those who are slaves in Egypt are not their own master but slaves to evil and sin and the things of this world that rule them. Those entrapped in Egypt have no hope except that a "deliverer" might come and set them free. He did. He has. Jesus came to set us free from the power of sin and declared that sin no longer had dominion over us.

For sin shall not be your Master, because you are not under law, but under grace (Romans 6:14).

Jesus Christ fulfilled the requirement of the law which demands death as a payment for sin. Romans 6:23 tells us that the wages (or price) of sin is death. God instituted the death penalty for sin when He established His standard for life. Through the acts of Adam and Eve, sin and the penalty for sin was introduced. They opened the door to the corruption of our human nature by disobeying God. Come with me to the garden and let's revisit the story for a moment to look at the "truth" of their act of rebellion.

In the Garden

The garden was the place where Adam and Eve enjoyed the presence of God. He walked with them and talked with them on a daily basis. They enjoyed an intimate friendship with God. God made known to Adam and Eve the standards of the "garden". In the garden God established many trees but two were extremely significant. The first tree was the "tree of life." This tree probably was associated with eternal life as best we can see from other scriptures (Genesis 3:22, Revelations 2:7). The second tree was the "tree of the knowledge of good and evil." This was the only tree that God commanded them not to eat from. Some theologians suggest that this tree was set as a test for man to see if he would obey God. God told Adam and Eve if they ate of this tree they would die (Genesis 3:17). Obedience to God was the standard in the garden; death was the penalty for disobedience.

Satan seized an opportunity to attack back at God by visiting His creation in the garden. Through crafty, deceptive conversation, and misrepresentation of truth Satan, disguised as a serpent, told Adam and Eve that God did not really mean what He said about dying if they ate from the tree (Genesis 3:4). Believing the lie, Adam and Eve succumbed to this story of deceit and ate the fruit of the tree. Suddenly they became aware of themselves. Isn't it interesting that before, they were only aware of God, and after, they were aware of themselves? They realized they were naked before God. They quickly sought a covering. Don't we all? They wanted to cover up their nakedness; their exposure. Sin does that. It makes us naked and exposed before God. It also makes us want to hide. Adam and Eve hid from God. They felt afraid and uncomfortable in His presence knowing that they had displeased Him. In this condition, they found it impossible to draw near God.

We are no different. The consciousness of our sinfulness causes us to run, to hide, and even to shun God. We too, know we have displeased Him. Hidden in the thicket of the Garden, they heard the footsteps of God. The Lord called out to them and asked a question, "Where are you?" Push pause and let's stop here for a moment. The question on the table is "Where are you?" Let me assure you this was **not** a geographical question. The all-knowing, all-seeing, everywhere God was **not** wondering where Adam and Eve were. I believe it was a spiritual question in nature. When God asked, "Where are you?" it was **not** because He did not know, but perhaps because He wanted Adam and Eve to know. Perhaps He wanted them to take inventory of where they were. They looked around and realized at that moment they were separated from God. They were not in the close proximity they had been accustomed. They were hidden away from God. Their act of disobedience had driven them to hide. Some say it was the original hide and seek – man hides and God seeks.

Nevertheless, God demanded man to answer up. Man blamed woman; woman blamed serpent. God dealt with the serpent (a.k.a Satan) first. He cursed the serpent to crawling on his belly, eating dust all the days of his life (Genesis 3:14). It's the position Satan would remain in until the crushing blow from Jesus would come years later (John 3:8). Now God dealt with man. Let's listen in.

And the Lord God said, "The man has now become like one of *us* knowing good and evil. He must not be allowed to reach out his hand and take also from the tree of life and eat and live forever" (Genesis 3:22; emphasis mine).

The Father, Son, and Holy Spirit were in conversation about the fate of disobedient man. The act of Adam and Eve set up independence from God. It also broke the intimate relationship God and man had once experienced. Man's sinfulness had separated him even physically from God's presence. Practically speaking man believed Satan when he told him that he could do what he wanted and not die. Can't you just hear him, "Hey, I know God said that you'd die, but He won't back it up. He loves you." It is true that God loves us. He loves us so much that He will not lie to us. When God said, "Don't break my command, or you will die." He meant it. God would not look away, nor dismiss such an act of rebellion.

So the Lord God banished him from the Garden of Eden .... After He drove the man out, He placed on the east side of the Garden of Eden, cherubim and a flaming sword flashing back and forth to guard the way to the tree of life (Genesis 3:23-24).

God keeps His word. I've often wondered why there was such a guarding of the tree of life. Was it perhaps no longer God's desire that man would live forever in such a fallen condition? Nevertheless, God enforced the penalty of sin...death! The word "death" as used here in the Old Testament literally means "everlasting destruction and *shut out of the presence of God"* (2 Kings 17:18, Genesis 4:14, 2 Thessalonians 1:9). It became the "death sentence" of every rebellious, sinful man. Satan lied to man and deceived man into believing that he could disobey God and still enjoy life with God. It's a lie to this day that man often believes.

Adam had been warned that he would die if he "transgressed," that is, disobeyed, God. God left Adam with the deliberate choice to believe Him and obey or disbelieve, disobey and die! It would require faith in God on Adam's part, to believe that what God had said He would do – He would do. But Satan came "a singing" and whistled a tune of deceit. He twisted truth and enticed man to try on for the first time the "coat of rebellion." He's still whistling the same ole tune and he has caused many (even in the church today) to believe they can rebel and nothing will happen. But the Bible says, "God is not a man that He should lie," and He doesn't! Disobedience brings death (separation) even today for those who have no way to pay for the penalty of sin. The price of sin has been set and it is high—death! Such banishment from the presence of God eternally is the reality of every unredeemed man. If sin has such a high price, we need to understand sin better. The Bible defines sin as a "transgression," "a wrongdoing" against God.[1]The root of sin is selfishness, that is, a grasping of things or pleasures for ourselves, regardless of the welfare of others and the commandments of God. [2] Ultimately, sin has become the refusal to be subject to God and His word. Sin is rooted in corrupt human desire.

When tempted, no one should say, "God is tempting me." For God cannot be tempted by evil, nor does He tempt anyone; but each one is tempted when, *by His own evil desire,* **He is dragged away and enticed. Then after desire has conceived, it gives birth to sin; and sin, when it is full grown, gives birth to death (James 1:13-15; emphasis mine).**

The deliberate decision by Adam and Eve to sin opened the door to the corruption of our human nature. This door has been open ever since. This corruption of human nature involves the innate desire to have what I want when I want it. It is fed by the enticement, the "dangling of the apple" kind of stuff that feeds our pleasure and not our obedience to God.

When woman saw that the fruit of the tree was good for food and pleasing to the eye and also desirable for gaining wisdom, she took some and ate it (Genesis 3:6).

Never mind that it was "off limits" by God, Eve was gratifying the cravings of her own desire. She was defiling herself by going after, "lusting after" what her eyes saw. And what her eyes saw she wanted. Perhaps that is why Jesus said in Matthew 5:29, **"If your right eye causes you to sin, gouge it out and throw it away. It is better for you to lose one part of your body than for your whole body to be thrown into hell."** No where in the Bible does God condemn a person for a thought Satan may place or that suddenly comes into a person's mind. However, God knows such thoughts can be accompanied by the approval of one's corrupted will, when enticed to consider the desire. Eve considered the thought so long, she partook. The thought birthed a desire, the desire birthed an action, the action birthed sin, and the sin led the way to death, the banishment from the garden, shut out of God's presence. This is why James warns us about sin that leads to death (James 1:14-16). Death—"separation from God"— can begin with a thought! The Bible teaches us to bring all thoughts captive, that is, in line with the will of God. All thoughts must be measured by God's yardstick (what He says). Any thoughts that fall short need to be abandoned. Oh, if it were only that easy.

Years ago in Vacation Bible School, I was taught to sing this song of truth. Perhaps you sang it too. "Be careful little eyes what you see. Oh, be careful little eyes what you see. For the Father up above is looking down with love, so be careful little eyes what you see." The second verse warned our ears to be careful what they hear. Verse three said "be careful little feet where you go." It's a song worth remembering. Paul warned us to not be ignorant of the schemes of the devil. He comes at us through our weaknesses. Little portals (open doors) in our lives where he entices us and causes us to fall— miss the mark (the standard) of God. It is sin at entry level. It all began in the garden and has been going on ever since. If that were the end of the story we would all be condemned to death, shut out of the presence of God. But it was not the end of the story, it was just the beginning.

God's plan for man has always included redemption (a payment for man's sin). Every rebellious, sinful man and woman has a need to be saved from such death. God will not change the penalty for death that He instituted. What He said He will do – He will do! But out of His matchless love, and His unfathomable mercy, He provides the payment of the penalty that He Himself imposed. God sent His very own Son to pay such a price. He would die in the place of every condemned man and woman thus fulfilling the requirement of death for sin. It was out of such an incredible love for His creation that God's plan would take such an extreme measure.

For God so loved the world that He gave His only son, so that everyone who believes in Him will not perish, but have eternal life. God did not send His son into the world to condemn the world, but to save the world through Him (John 3:16).

Matthew 20:8 says that Jesus came **"to give His life as a ransom for many."** The word ransom conveys the meaning of a price paid to obtain the freedom of others. Jesus paid the price for the freedom of those "guilty of sin." He paid with His life and all who accepted such a payment on their behalf would be "saved"— spared the death penalty. Our part is to accept Jesus as our payment and surrender the reigns of our life to Him declaring Him Lord. The word "Lord" means having power, dominion, authority and the right to master. Instead of being such a slave to sin, condemned to die, we would now be set free to live. As a result we are to….

Offer (ourselves) to God, as those who have been brought from death to life; and offer the parts of (our) body to Him as instruments of righteousness. For sin shall not be (our) master, because you (we) are not under the law, but under grace. You (we) have been set free from sin and have become slaves to righteousness. Just as you used to offer the parts of your body in slavery to impurity and to ever increasing wickedness, so now offer them in slavery of righteousness leading to holiness. When you were slaves to sin you were free

from control of righteousness. What benefit did you reap at that time from the things you are now ashamed of? Those things result in death. But now that you have been set free from sin and have become slaves to God, the benefit you reap leads to holiness, and the result is eternal life. For the wages of sin is death, but the gift of God is eternal life in Christ Jesus our Lord (Romans 6:13-14, 18-23; parenthesis mine).

In Galatians 2:20, Paul puts it another way:

"I have been crucified with Christ and I no longer live, but Christ lives in me. The life I live in the body, I live by faith in the Son of God who loved me and *gave himself for me*" (emphasis mine).

Christ died so that our sins would be forgiven. Forgiveness means "to cover," "to pardon," "to cancel," "to send away." [3] It's the very "covering" Adam and Eve needed. It is indeed the "covering" we need too. Forgiveness is necessary because we **all** sin and fall short of the glory of God (Romans 3:23). Our sin destroys our relationship with God, exposes us as naked, with no covering and can lead to eternal banishment from the presence of God. But through Jesus' death, the shedding of His blood as evidence, we now have a covering that cancels and pardons our sin.

In order to receive such forgiveness and such a covering there must be repentance; confession of our sin. The word repentance has often been taught as a "turning around" or "turning away from" one's sin. This is true. However, the more literal meaning of "repent" is to be "re-penitent" or "again humble". One who is penitent expresses humble or regretful pain or sorrow for sins or offenses. To repent means to come back to that place of humility and sorrow over sin.[4] It is the place in our lives, where we declare our need for a savior, a redeemer, and a deliverer. It is the place where we confess, "agree with God," and acknowledge our sin. It is the place where we get truthful about our rebellion to His will. It's the place where each must take ownership for the "biting of the apple." Such repentance, humbleness, and sorrow for our sin, and agreement with God's word about our sin, requires faith; faith that Jesus is the way back into God's presence. It requires faith that His death is the restoring work of our relationship with God. Such faith involves accepting Christ not only as payment for the penalty of sin, but also as Lord of our life. Repentance actually involves a change of lords— from the lordship of Satan (Ephesians 2:2) to the lordship of Christ and His word (Acts 26:18). [5] Satan is the ruler of the world and all without Christ are under his control and enslaved to his power. But those who place their faith in Jesus are delivered, set free from Satan's control and lordship. The Bible makes it clear, **"that now you are free from the power of sin and are slaves of God and His benefits to you include holiness and everlasting life"** (Romans 6:22).

If you have repented of your sins and become sorrowful of your wrongdoing before God and if you have confessed and acknowledged such sins and you have received Jesus' payment for your sins …. My friend, *shake a leg, you're free!"*

For whom the Son sets free, is free indeed (John 8:36).

Chapter 3

"Somebody Ought to Yell Fire!"

Examine yourselves to see whether you are in the faith....
(2 Corinthians 13:5a)

I must confess that when I started writing this book, I didn't really want to spend a lot of time on what is considered the basic components of Christianity, such as repentance, confession, and salvation. I really wanted to get on with the "meat" of the book, the deliverance of the church from bondage. I felt like most Christians knew the basics and mere mention would be sufficient. It was at this crossroads of chapter three that God reminded me of the two reasons the church is in bondage – *they don't know truth or they don't apply truth*. The truth is some Christians have been sold a cheap salvation. So cheap in fact, that it is not salvation at all. They have received a salvation that says you can be Christian and still live any way you want. Such Christianity – such salvation – is not backed up anywhere in scripture. True salvation demands a change. A change of who's in charge, a change of who leads and who follows. Many call Jesus Savior, but don't allow Him to be Lord. They continue to run their own lives and insist on doing things their own way. The Bible makes it clear we cannot call Him Lord and be in charge at the same time! Jesus puts it this way:

"Why do you call me 'Lord, Lord' and do not do what I say?"
(Luke 6:46)

True salvation will demand changes in our lifestyles, behaviors, attitudes, language, and anything else about us that is not Christ-like. Salvation is the beginning point of a transforming work of God by His Holy Spirit in the life of every believer to make us more like Jesus.

For years, I believed I was Christian when, indeed, I was not. At the young age of nine, I had responded to an invitation at the end of a revival service at our church. I went down front with several others, mainly my friends. I was asked several questions about my desire to become a Christian. I responded with the expected 'yeses.' I know one of the questions was, "Do you earnestly and sincerely, repent of your sins?" I said, "Yes." It was the expected response, but I had not repented of anything. Only moments earlier, I had decided to go down the aisle! I really had no idea what questions would be asked of me, but, when put on the spot, I said yes. No one led me in a prayer of repentance. For me, it was a "mouth thing," not a "heart thing." Maybe my motives for going forward were pure, but my response was not. Some would argue that I cannot point to that single experience and verify that I was not saved. Maybe this is true. However, I can point to the life that followed. The Bible teaches very succinctly that there should be "evidences of salvation." Such evidences are the true test of salvation. God wants us to have assurance of our salvation. I had none.

True salvation is based on grace and faith— God's grace which is His undeserved favor to save us, and our faith to believe in and respond to the Saving One. Such faith must be demonstrated in a personal response to the Savior. Faith in Jesus Christ is the only requirement of God for salvation. However, such faith is not mere head knowledge of who Jesus is and what He did. Such faith is "heart knowledge."

That if you confess with your mouth "Jesus is Lord," and *believe in your heart* that God raised Him from the dead, you will be saved (Romans 10:9; emphasis mine).

As best I see it there are two components of salvation: confession out of your mouth that Jesus is Lord **and** belief in your heart that God raised Him from the dead. In other words, He is the Risen Savior, the Living Christ. The Bible also points to the fact that the condition of the heart to receive salvation is repentance. When Peter was preaching on the day of Pentecost he said:

"God has made this Jesus whom you crucified, both Lord and Christ." When the people heard this, they were cut to the heart and said to Peter and the other apostles, 'Brothers, What shall we do?' Peter replied, 'Repent and be baptized, every one of you, in the name of Jesus Christ for the forgiveness of your sins. And you will receive the gift of the Holy Spirit" (Acts 2:36b – 38).

In another scripture Jesus himself said it this way:

"This is what is written: The Christ will suffer and rise from the dead on the third day, and *repentance and forgiveness* **of sins will be preached in His name to all nations, beginning at Jerusalem" (Luke 24:46-47; emphasis mine).**

When speaking on another occasion, Jesus simply said, **"Unless you repent, you too will all perish" (Luke 13:3).** John the Baptist was the forerunner with the message. He came preaching repentance. It was a preparing work of the heart for the salvation that would soon come through Jesus Christ. His message was simple and to the point, **"Repent, for the kingdom of heaven is near."** He was sent to prepare hearts to receive Jesus. Repentance was the preparation. Repentance is not the reciting of words. Repentance is a work in the heart that turns it away from sin and towards Jesus. As I wrote in Chapter Two, the literal meaning of repentance is "repent or "to again be penitent," which means humbled or sorrowful. One who is re- penitent expresses humble sorrow or regretful pain for sins and offenses. Such a broken state of the heart is the catalyst, if you will, for the "turning to" the only One that can save us from the penalty of our sins. A repentant heart is the heart prepared to receive the gift of salvation.

Confession that Jesus is Lord is also essential to salvation (Romans 10:9). The understanding of that confession, I believe, is equally essential. It is my opinion that you should not confess nor commit to what you do not understand. It is not essential that you fully understand Jesus at this point, but that you understand confession and commitment to Jesus. God will spend the next however many years of your life bringing you into the wonderful revelation of who Jesus is. On this side of heaven none of us can fully know or understand all there is to know about Jesus (1 Corinthians 13:12). That is the journey of our confession and commitment.

The earliest creed or confessions of the New Testament was not Jesus as Savior, but Jesus as Lord.[1] Jesus Christ is specifically called Savior 16 times in the New Testament and Lord more than 450 times. No one can receive Him as Savior without receiving Him as Lord. It is an essential ingredient of salvation. As explained in Chapter two, the word Lord means having power, dominion, authority and the right to master. To confess "Jesus is Lord" is not an outward profession, but an inward sincere surrender of the heart to be ruled and mastered by Jesus. It is the giving over of control of one's life and declaring Jesus in charge. The word confess, means to own, acknowledge or publicly declare a belief in and an adherence to. Such confession of Jesus as Master, authority of our life, is inseparable from salvation. We speak this confession out of our mouth because repentance has brought us to the place that we realize apart from Jesus we have no hope of deliverance from our bondage to sin where sin has been the master, ruler and power of our life. A repentant, broken heart cries out and invites Jesus to take over the reins.

Such would be the case of my life 20 years after going down front in that revival service. The summation of my life during that 20 year span can only be expressed as lost and bound. I was surely in Egypt and sin was my master. Even though I sat in church every Sunday with my name on the roll, I had no concept and no conviction of the Holy Spirit. I was definitely and defiantly in charge. Upon entering the decade of my twenties, I was a "pro" at driving my life. I drove wherever I wanted, whenever I wanted, with little regard to God, His standard or anyone else's. I reasoned that I deserved happiness and could do whatever it took to get it. I made some horrible decisions to go after what I thought was "greener grass." My gold did not glitter and turned out it was only "fool's gold" all along. Like Eve, I did what pleased me and pursued the things my eyes desired. Status and titles were real important to me during those years, as was the need to be needed. Being a "perfectionist" in demeanor did not help my cause. I even did bad things perfectly!

It wasn't until my own sin finally became a noose around my neck that I realized the reckless driving of my life was going to kill me. Much injury had already occurred when one day I found myself sitting at the crash site of my soul. I was suffering greatly and causing others to suffer with me. Sitting in the heap of my mangled life I finally cried out to God with such an intensity heaven couldn't miss it. In my own sarcastic, yet broken way, I yelled at the top of my lungs, "God, I give up. If you think you can do any better then be my guest. I surrender." Heaven must have breathed a sigh of relief, because one bound soul was about to get set free. Just a few months later after hearing a message about true repentance and salvation, I knelt beside my bed and asked Jesus into my heart. Godly sorrow overwhelmed me about the life I had been living, the choices that I had made and the people I had hurt. I cried from the bottom of my being. Such tears were not wasted. God caught every one of them and began to cleanse and carry away the filth of living in Egypt – my "sin city" for so long.

Upon hearing the message of repentance and salvation, I believed in Jesus and wanted Jesus to do for me what I could not do for myself. I could not free myself *from* myself, my sin, or my adversary. I was caught, bound, and entangled and could not get free. But God opened my ears and what I heard and understood for the first time was "Whom the Son sets free is free indeed." I desired such freedom and realized at that moment Jesus was the way out. I was tired of the weight of the chains of bondage. So I decided to trust Jesus, by turning over the control of my life to Him. Spiritually, we changed seats. He would now drive and I would now ride. It's a decision I have never regretted. Jesus became Lord of my life. Sin was no longer my master – He was! My sorrow over my sin turned my heart toward Jesus and made salvation possible. It was the first time such a freeing, cleansing, saving work had been done. I had been saved, forgiven of my sin and my past, and I knew it.

What followed was an intense desire to change my ways. It did not happen all at once, but there were several habits and behaviors I did have to separate from initially. God showed me that these habits and behaviors were feeding my lifestyle of sin. I surrendered my life to the direction, guidance and authority of Jesus and He began to walk me out of Egypt by a path that He alone knew. He is indeed "the way!" I have been following Jesus for some 18 years and I can truthfully say our walk together gets better every day!

There is salvation in no one else! There is no other name in all of heaven for people to call on to save them (Acts 4:12 New Living Translation).

Only Jesus has the power to save! His name is the only one in all the world that can save anyone (Acts 4:12 Contemporary English Version).

I am the Way, the Truth, and the Life (John 14:6).

The second component of our salvation is, "**Believing in our heart that God raised Jesus from the dead" (Romans 10:9).** Biblically, the heart is the center of our emotions, intellect, and will. It is a very different place than the mind. The mind is the place of reasoning and thinking. It's the place where facts are often processed, but this would not be the place that God would reveal salvation. It would not be a "head thing" based on facts, but a "heart thing", based on faith. Salvation can only be appreciated by faith. Faith is the activity of a heart being redeemed. Faith means believing, trusting, relying and adhering to Jesus. Such faith is both the act of a single moment and the continuing attitude that must grow and be strengthened. The essential component of our faith is the belief in the raising of Jesus from the dead. Christian salvation hangs on the work of the cross. It is the place God displays His full plan to redeem man. It is the central event in salvation. It is the place where our death penalty is paid in full and declared null and void.

The resurrection of Jesus is the assurance of the breaking of the chains of sin and the freedom to walk in newness of life. Jesus paid the price and paved the way. The way leads to the cross, the burial, and the resurrection of Jesus. Every believer must accept the way of this redemptive plan or salvation is not possible. The importance of such "belief in the heart" stems from the implication it has for each who accepts Jesus' payment for their sin.

But if it is preached that Christ has been raised from the dead, how can some of you say that there is no resurrection of the dead? If there is no resurrection of the dead, then not even Christ has been raised. And if Christ has not been raised, our preaching is useless and so is your faith. More than that, we are then found to be false witnesses about God, for we have testified about God that He raised Christ from the dead. But He did not raise Him, if in fact the dead are not raised. For if the dead are not raised, then Christ has not been raised either. And if Christ has not been raised your faith is futile; you are still in your sins. Then those also who have fallen asleep in Christ are lost. If only for this life, we have hope in Christ, we are to be pitied more than all men. But Christ has indeed been raised from the dead, the first fruits of those who have fallen asleep. For since death came through a man, the resurrection of the dead, comes through a man. For as in Adam all die, so in Christ all live (1 Corinthians 15:12-19).

Now I know that's some wordy scripture, but Paul was going into great detail because some were denying that Jesus had been raised from the dead. It was essential not only for the church to understand but believe in their hearts that God did what He said He would do or there was no living Christ, which is the basis of our faith. Paul was reminding them that they came into such a saving faith, believing God had indeed raised Jesus from the dead, and that He is indeed now the Living Christ. I like the way *The Message* translation puts it.

If you became believers because you trusted the proclamation that Christ is alive, risen from the dead, how can you let people say (to you) that there is no such thing as a resurrection? If there's no resurrection, there's no Living Christ. And face it –

if there's no resurrection for Christ everything we've told you is smoke and mirrors, and everything you've staked your life on is smoke and mirrors. Not only that, but we would be guilty of a string of barefaced lies about God, all these affidavits we passed on to you verifying that God raised up Christ – sheer fabrications, if there's no resurrection.

If corpses can't be raised, the Christ wasn't because He was indeed dead. And if Christ wasn't raised, then all you're doing is wandering about in the dark, as lost as ever. It's even worse for those who die hoping in Christ and resurrection because they're already in the grave. If all we get out of Christ is a little inspiration for a few short years here on earth we're a pretty sorry lot. But the truth is that Christ has been raised up, the first in a long legacy of those who are going to leave the cemeteries. There is a nice symmetry in this. Death initially came by man, and resurrection from death came by man. Everybody dies in Adam; everybody comes alive in Christ (1 Corinthians 15:12-22).

Then, I especially love the way *The Message* translation puts verse 29 of this same chapter:

If there's no chance of resurrection for a corpse, if God's power stops at the cemetery gates, why do we keep doing things that suggest he's going to clean the place out someday, pulling everyone up on their feet alive?

Good question! Paul goes on to answer it by saying he does what he does, preaching the gospel (the life, death, and resurrection of Christ) because He is convinced of Christ's resurrection and also yours and mine! The Bible says that the very same power that raised Christ from the dead will also raise us (Romans 8:11). The alternate belief is only this— We eat, we drink, and then we die. And that's all there is to it. But Jesus overcame death and its destructive power and became a living example of life after death for those who follow Him in faith. Jesus' triumph over the death verdict brings hope for every believer. Death does not have the final say for those who are "in Christ." Believers do not have to fear death physically or spiritually. God's power does not stop at the cemetery gates!

It was sin that made death so frightening and law-code guilt that gave sin its leverage, its destructive power. But now in a single victorious stroke of life, all three – sin, guilt, death are gone, the gift of our Master, Jesus Christ. Thank God (1 Corinthians 15:56; *The Message*).

This is why we can say with all the saints, **"Death swallowed by triumphant Life! Who got the last word, oh Death? Oh, Death, who's afraid of you now? (1 Corinthians 15:55; *The Message*)**

Salvation brings the believer the hope of, and one day the reality of, eternal life. The Bible says, **"It is appointed once for man to die, then the judgment"** (Hebrews 9:27). It is important that we "believe in our heart," and wrap our lives around this aspect of our salvation, because what we believe will determine how we live and how we live determines where we will spend eternity. Resurrection of our earthly bodies will come. "All will be pulled up on their feet alive," as the translation reads. It is at this point that death will be defeated for every believer. The fact will become reality that "though we died, yet we shall live." Believers will then follow Christ into eternity. Death is indeed swallowed by triumphant life.

It is not enough to just believe in Jesus, *even Satan* believes in Jesus, God requires confession, a declaration, a belief in, and adherence to, Jesus as Lord.[2] Such a confession is inseparable from salvation and such confession is directly tied to "belief in our heart" of the living Christ, the resurrected Savior.

For with the heart a person believes (adheres to, trust in, and relies on Christ) and so is justified (declared righteous, acceptable to God) and with the mouth he confesses (declares openly and speaks out freely his faith) and confirms (his) salvation (Romans 10:10; *Amplified Bible*).

For those who make such confession and surrendering of their lives to Jesus through repentance for their sins, accompanied by belief in their heart, the salvation work begins. The sincerity of one's "saving" experience is evidenced by marked, apparent, noticeable changes in one's life. The Bible calls these "expected" changes "evidences of salvation." Salvation does not leave one in the same state in which they were found. True salvation demands change. You cannot stay like you are and go with God. The old must be shed so the new can come forth.

If anyone is in Christ he is a new creation, the old has gone the new has come (2 Corinthians 5:11).

Evidences of Salvation

I write these things to you who believe in the name of the son of God so that you may *know* that you have eternal life (1 John 5:13; emphasis mine).

Every Christian can have the assurance of their salvation; that is, the certainty that they will spend eternity in heaven. Such assurance comes from what the Bible refers to as evidences of salvation. No knowledge is as important to believers as the certainty that they have eternal life.

Examine yourselves to see whether you are in the faith; test yourselves. Do you not realize that Christ Jesus is in you – unless of course you fail the test? (2 Corinthians 13:5)

All professing Christians should examine themselves to determine that their salvation is a present reality. Such testing of one's faith is laid out in the book of 1 John. John reveals five specific tests by which believers may know with assurance that they have eternal life. The tests are as follows:
1. The test of faith and fellowship with Christ
2. The test of an obedience that keeps Christ's commands
3. The test of holy living, i.e. turning from sin to fellowship with God

4. The test of love for God and other believers
5. The test of the Spirit's witness

(1) The Test of Faith and Fellowship with Christ

If we claim to have fellowship with him (Jesus) yet walk in the darkness, we lie and do not live by the truth. But if we walk in the light, as he is in the light, we have fellowship with one another, and the blood of Jesus purifies us from all sin (1 John 1:6).

The word "fellowship" as used in the scripture means "having in common." The phrase "to walk in darkness" means to live in sin and immoral pleasure. Christians cannot claim fellowship with Christ and live continually in sin and immorality at the same time. If we claim that we experience such a shared life with Him and live in such a state, the Bible says we are liars. The very essence of the word salvation means "deliverance," "bringing safely through," and "keeping from harm." Salvation pulls us out of the miry clay (sinful living) and sets our "feet upon the rock" (righteous living through Jesus). Such salvation, delivers us from bondage— the continual captivity of sin in our lives. Salvation does not demand perfection this side of heaven, but it does demand response. Our response must be to sincerely follow and live for Christ. "To walk in darkness" or "to live in sin" in today's vernacular is best understood as one who makes a practice of sin. The Bible says it this way:

No one who lives in Him keeps on sinning. No one who continues to sin has either seen Him or knows Him. Dear children, do not let anyone lead you astray. He who does what is right is righteous, just as He is righteous. He who does what is sinful is of the devil, because the devil has been sinning from the beginning. The reason the son of God appeared was to destroy the devil's work. No one who is born of God will continue to sin, because God's seed remains in him; he cannot go on sinning because he has been born of God (1 John 3:6-9).

The verb "to sin" is a present active infinitive implying *continued action*. John is emphasizing that those *truly* born of God cannot make sin their way of life, because God's life cannot exist in those who practice sin. For people to have God's life in them and to go on sinning (in a continued way) is a spiritual impossibility.[3] Believers may occasionally lapse from God's standard, but they will not continue in sin. That which keeps the faithful from sinning is God's seed in them, that is, God's very life, the Holy Spirit. By faith, the indwelling Spirit of Christ, and the word of God, all believers can live moment by moment free from offense and sin. It is possible!

The Bible generally distinguishes between different kinds of sins; unintentional sins (Leviticus 4:2, 13, 22, Leviticus 5:4-6, Numbers 15:22-29), less serious sins (Matthew 5:19), deliberate sins (1 John 5:16-17) and sins bringing spiritual death (1 John 5:16). But don't misunderstand because they are all still sin! John stresses that there are certain sins that born again believers will not commit because of the eternal life of Christ abiding in them (1 John 2:11, 15 – 16, 3:6 – 10, 14-15, 4:20, 5:2, 2 John 9). These sins, because of the gravity and origin in nature, indicate an intense rebellion against God. Examples, that give conclusive evidence that one is still in bondage to wickedness and sin are murder (1 John 3:15, 2:11); sexual impurity or immorality (Romans 1:21-22, 1 Corinthians 5:11, Ephesians 5:5, Revelation 21:8); abandonment of one's family (1 Timothy 5:8); leading others into sin (Matthew 18:6-10); and cruelty (Matthew 24:48-51). These sins reveal utter rejection of honor towards God and loving care for others. Thus anyone who says, "*I have fellowship with Jesus Christ, am indwelt by the Spirit, and am in a saving relationship with Him,*" yet participates in the above mentioned sins, is deceiving himself and "*is a liar and the truth is not in him.*" Sins coming from a rebellious disposition against God and His word will bring us under judgment and spiritual death *unless we confess them* and repent through faith in Jesus Christ. [4] All sins, even the less serious, or unintended ones, *can* lead to a weakening of our spiritual life, if not checked.

As New Testament believers, we continually need Christ's atoning blood to cover mistakes, weaknesses and unintentional failings that flow from the frailty of our human nature. The blood of Jesus that purifies us from all sins refers to an ongoing work known as sanctification. Part of the work of sanctification is the continual cleansing and purifying work of the Holy Spirit in believers through repentance and confession. It allows us to have intimate fellowship with Christ.

But if we walk in the light, as he is in the light, we have fellowship with one another and the blood of Jesus, his son, purifies us from all sin (1 John 1:7).

"Walking in the light" means to walk in the truth of God as revealed in His Word and to make *a sincere and sustained* effort by His grace to follow it in word and deed. Eternal life is not secured and maintained merely by an act of repentance and faith occurring in the past. It involves, also a present living union and fellowship with Christ.

Examine yourselves to see whether you are in the faith.... *(2 Corinthians 13:5a)*

(2) The Test of Obedience that Keeps Christ's Commands

We know that we have come to know him *if we obey* his commands. The man who says, "I know him," but does not do what He commands is a liar and the truth is not in him (1 John 2:3-4; emphasis mine).

The second test of assurance of salvation is the test of obedience. In the early church a teaching circulated that caused grave misunderstanding of grace and salvation. The teaching was that the forsaking of a sinful life was optional for the believer. Such "teachers" taught that one can legitimately claim to "know" God in a saving relationship and at the same time be indifferent or disobedient to God's will and commands .[5] Those who make such a claim are liars, and those who believe such claims have been deceived. There are those who would say such a statement is ludicrous and yet live it. Obeying the commands of Christ is **not** optional for those who would have eternal life. Obedience to Christ, *though never perfect*, must nevertheless be genuine. It is an essential aspect of saving faith that comes from our love for him. Without love for Christ, trying to obey his commands, becomes legalism (a list of to do's!). Love is the motivation for such obedience.

"If you *love* me, you will obey what I command" (John 14:15).

The true test of our love for Christ is our obedience to Christ.

"Whoever has my commands and obeys them, he is the one who loves me" (John 14:21).

In Matthew 7:21-23, Jesus puts it in stronger language.

Not everyone who says to me, "Lord, Lord," will enter the kingdom of heaven, but only he who does the will of my father who is in heaven. Many will say to me on that day, 'Lord, Lord, did we not prophesy in your name and in your name drive out demons and perform many miracles?' Then I will tell them plainly, "I never knew you. Away from me, you evil doers."

Jesus emphatically taught that carrying out the will and command of His heavenly Father was a condition of entering the kingdom of heaven. This does not tie salvation to works or anything of our own effort, because God *always* makes available the obedience He demands of us. It's part of the 'gift' in the plan of salvation. God will never demand more of you than what He gives. **"For it is God who works in you, to will and to act according to His good purpose" (Philippians 2:13)**. The grace (un-merited favor of God) of salvation is at work in the life of the believer to produce both the desire *and* the power to do His will. But God's work is not one of compulsion. Such a work of grace within us is always dependent on our *cooperation*. However, God's gift of such grace does not nullify human responsibility or action. But because of the grace supplied, we *are* capable of doing God's will and obeying His commands. It is an "obedience that comes from faith" (Romans 1:5). [6] True faith in

God always manifests itself in obedience to God.

What use is it, my brother, if someone says he has faith but he has no works? Can that faith save him? If it does not have works (deeds and actions of obedience to back up) by itself, is destitute of power (inoperative, dead) (James 2:14, 17; *Amplified Bible***).**

Our faith in God is tied inseparably to our obedience to God. Saving faith is always a living faith that does not stop with mere confession of Christ as Savior, but also prompts obedience to Him as Lord. Obedience is an essential of faith in Jesus Christ [7].

> *Examine yourselves to see whether you are in the faith....*
> *(2 Corinthians 13:5 a)*

(3) The Test of Holy living, that is, the turning away from sin to fellowship with God.

The scripture reads, **"But just as He who called you is holy, so be holy in all you do; for it is written: 'Be holy, because I am holy' " (1 Peter 1:16).** The third test of assurance of salvation is that of Holy living. God is holy and calls His people who represent Him to be holy. **"Make every effort to live in peace with all men and to be holy, without holiness no one will see the Lord" (Hebrews 12:14).**

Salvation involves a work of God in the life of every believer. Such a work is called sanctification. Sanctification by definition means "to make holy, to consecrate, to separate from the world, to be set apart from sin", so that we may have intimate fellowship with God. [8] You cannot "get holy" on your own! But you are expected as a believer to surrender to the work of God in your life. Such a sanctifying work is the job of the Holy Spirit. It is by His bidding that we are beckoned out of worldly ways, ungodly behavior, language, attitudes or relationships. It is the power of the Holy Spirit within to enable us to walk away from temptation. It is also the convicting work of the Holy Spirit that causes us to repent when we fail. True salvation demands surrender to such ongoing sanctifying work of the Holy Spirit. Such ongoing work is the purifying process of our hearts that leads to holiness – the holiness God desires in each of us. Hear again 1 John 1:16:

If we claim to have fellowship with Him yet walk in the darkness, (to live in sin and immoral pleasure) we lie and do not live by the truth (*Amplified Bible*).

A present saving grace is evidenced by the truth of God in our life. It is His truth that comes in and releases us from our bondage to sin. It is such truth that propels us out of darkness into His marvelous light. Truth that demands we separate ourselves from the ungodly ways of this world.

Mankind was created in the image of God (Genesis 1:26). Such an "image" would reflect the love, glory, and the holiness of God. On the basis of this "image" and "likeness" to God, man and woman could have fellowship with God. It was only through the fall of mankind in the garden that the moral likeness to God was broken. In the beginning, Adam and Eve were sinless and holy, possessing wisdom, love, and the will to do right. When Adam and Eve sinned, their moral likeness to God was corrupted. It is God's plan through redemption to restore the original likeness, the image He first desired and created.

You were taught with regard to your former way of life, to put off your old self, which is being corrupted by its deceitful desires; to be made new in the attitude of your minds; and to put on *the new self, created to be like God in true righteousness and holiness* **(Ephesians 4:24; emphasis mine).**

Sanctification is both a work of God and a work of His people. In order to accomplish God's will in sanctification, believers must participate in the Spirit's sanctifying work by "ceasing to do evil" (Romans 6:12), "purifying themselves from everything that contaminates body and spirit" (2 Corinthians 7:10), and "keeping themselves from being polluted by the world" (James 1:27). As we are instructed in the scriptures we are to make every *effort* to be holy. Such an effort is in the heeding of the Holy Spirit. The Holy Spirit knows the highway to holiness. It is His job to lead you there. It is your job to follow.

And do not grieve the Holy Spirit of God, with whom you were sealed for the day of redemption (Ephesians 4:30).

Believers grieve the Holy Spirit when they ignore His presence, His inner voice or His leading. Grieving the Holy Spirit can lead to resisting the Holy Spirit which in turn can lead to putting out the Spirit's fire in the life of the believer.

Those who live according to the sinful nature have their minds set on what that nature desires; but those who live in accordance with the Spirit have their minds set on what the Spirit desires (Romans 8:5).

To live "in accordance with the Spirit" is to seek and submit to the Holy Spirit's direction and enablement, and to concentrate on the things of God. [9] It is to live consciously and consistently in God's presence, *trusting* Him to give us the help and grace we need to accomplish His will in and through us. The Holy Spirit operates in our lives through internal warnings, impressions or nudges. Holy living comes by heeding the Holy Spirit.

Examine yourselves to see whether you are in the faith ....
(2 Corinthians 13:5a)

(4) The Test of love for God and other believers

The fourth test of the assurance as outlined in the book of first John is the test of love for God and other believers. Everything that God has done, is doing and will do is out of a love for His children so pure and so extravagant that the human heart cannot comprehend it all. The Bible bears testimony in scripture after scripture of God's great love for us.

For God so loved the world that He gave his only Son, that whoever believes in Him shall not perish but have eternal life (John 3:16).

This is how we know what love is: Jesus Christ laid down His life for us. And we ought to lay down our lives for our brother (1 John 3:16).

This is how God showed His love among us. He sent His one and only Son into the world that we might live through Him. This is love, not that we loved God, but that He loved us and sent His Son as an atoning sacrifice for our sins. We love because He first loved us (1 John 4:9-10, 19).

There never has been nor will there ever be, a love that can match the love of our heavenly Father. He gives such love unconditionally, but His heart cry is for us to love Him back. A reciprocated love is the key to an intimate relationship, the relationship God desires for us to have with Him. This love relationship is the one thing God wants from you. Everything about the Christian life hinges on our knowing and experiencing God's love and reciprocating by giving our love in return. It's the essence and evidence of our relationship with God. It's the greatest commandment of God.

Love the Lord your God with all your heart and with all your soul and with all your strength (Deuteronomy 6:5, Matthew 22:37, Mark 12:30).

When Jesus was asked what the greatest commandment was, the above scripture was the one He quoted, but He did not stop there.

Jesus replied, "Love the Lord your God with all your heart and with all your soul and with all your mind. This is the first and greatest commandment. And the second is like it: Love your neighbor as yourself. All the law and prophets hang on these two commandments" (Matthew 22:37-40).

Jesus tied our love for God to our love for others. In other words, we cannot love God and not love others. Our love for God demands an expression in loving others.

Anyone who claims to be in the light but hates his brother is still in darkness (1 John 2:9).

This is how we know who are the children of God are and who the children of the devil are. Anyone who does not do what is right is not a child of God; nor is anyone who does not love his brother (1 John 3:10).

And this is His command "to believe in the name of his Son, Jesus Christ, and to love one another as he commands" (1 John 3:2).

Everyone who believes that Jesus is the Christ is born of God, and everyone who loves the father loves His child as well. This is how we know that we love the children of God; by loving God and carrying out His commands (1 John 5:1-2).

Devoted love— it's the request of God for every believer. This kind of love starts in the heart of God and is given to His children that we may give it to one another. Such a devoted love comes from a desire birthed by the Holy Spirit in the heart of the believer when one surrenders to Jesus.

A new command I give you: "Love one another as I have loved you." As I have loved you, so you must love one another. By this all men will know you are my disciples, if you have love one for another (John 13:34-35).

Believers are commanded to love all people, even our enemies! (Matthew 5:44) They are called to especially love and esteem other believers (Galatians 6:10). Such love is not optional in the life of a believer. Salvation makes way for such a love to grow and to over-flow out of the heart of every believer. When the love *of* God and *for* God has earnestly grabbed your heart and life, it will be evidenced in love for others. Jesus says it will be our Christian moniker. It will be a tale tell sign of salvation because apart from God no one is able to love *all*. Only His love is so enabling and perfecting. Nowhere else can one find such love. Nowhere is such love in operation.

One of the ways the world will recognize Christians is by such love that cannot be produced by worthy or human endeavor. Such love must be preceded by a sincere devoted love for God— a love that places God first in our lives. Such love has a personal attachment of allegiance and loyalty to Him. Such love is expressed in dedication to His word, His will and His ways. Such love is evidence of the saving grace at work in the life of the believer. Apart from salvation, the redeeming work of God in our life, we cannot love Him or anyone else in such a way. God makes it clear that one of the ways we express our love for Him is by loving all others. First Corinthians 13, known as the Love chapter of the Bible, says without love we are like a "resounding gong and a clanging cymbal." God did not set religious activity as His hallmark— He set love. He set love above faith and hope (1 Corinthians 13:13). Love is the Christ- like character that is to mark the life of every believer. It is how the world will know "whose" we are. My friend let us love one another, for such love is an evidence of our salvation.

Examine yourselves to see whether you are in the faith....
(2 Corinthians 13:5a)

(5) The Test of the Spirit's Witness

We know that we live in Him and He in us because He has given us of His Spirit
(1 John 4:13).

But you have an anointing from the Holy One, and all of you know the truth. As for you the anointing you received from Him remains in you, and you do not need anyone to teach you.

But as His anointing teaches you about all things and as that anointing is real, not counterfeit – just as it has taught you remain in Him (1 John 2:20, 27).

The *Amplified Bible* expounds the word, anointing, as the "unction" of God, or the Holy Spirit within us. We can compare this scripture to John 4:26 and John 16:13 to verify.

But the Counselor, the Holy Spirit, whom the Father, will send in My name will teach you all things and remind you of everything I have said to you.

But when He, the Spirit of truth comes He will guide you in all truth. He will not speak on His own, He will speak only what He hears, and He will tell you what is yet to come.

A strong evidence of salvation in the life of a believer is the *inner witness* of the Holy Spirit. The scripture makes it clear that He is the unction, the anointing, and the divine sanctifying grace of God in our life that counsels, guides, and instructs us. He is the voice inside that speaks truth to us. He is the One who tells believers of things yet to come. God gives, as an evidence of salvation, His Spirit to every believer. The Holy Spirit is the enablement of God to walk out the Christian life. He is the power of God to overcome evil, temptation, and our own sin nature. He is the essence of God. He is what sets us apart from worldliness and carnality.

The Holy Spirit also brings about the necessary conviction; conviction of sin, righteousness and judgment. Jesus said,

When He comes, He will convict the world of guilt in regard to sin and righteousness and judgment; in regard to sin because men do not believe in me; in regard to righteousness because I am going to the Father, where you see me no longer; and in regard to judgment, because the prince of this world now stands condemned (John 16:8-11).

The word convict means "to expose, refute and convince." The

Holy Spirit operates the ministry of conviction in three areas— Sin, Righteousness and Judgment. All three are important in the life of the believer. In regard to the conviction of sin, the Holy Spirit will expose sin and unbelief in order to awaken a consciousness of guilt and the need for forgiveness. Such conviction leads to a choice of repentance and forgiveness. In regard to righteousness, the Holy Spirit makes us aware of God's standard of righteousness through the example of Jesus Christ. He is the standard for believers to follow. In regard to judgment, the Holy Spirit convinces people of Satan's defeat at the cross, God's judgment of the world, and the future judgment of the entire human race. [10] The convicting work of the Holy Spirit works in the lives of the believers in order to teach, correct, and guide them in all truth. The goal of His work is to reproduce Christ's Holy life in their lives and give each a sincere desire and disposition to obey God. [11] Such an inner witness and an inner work is a marker for every true believer of God. This witness of the Holy Spirit is an evidence of the saving grace; work of God, in a present every day real sort of way. The Holy Spirit is our guide on the road to a realized salvation when Jesus returns. The Spirit works within us to do what is necessary to awaken and deepen our awareness of Jesus' presence in our lives, drawing our hearts toward Him in faith, love, obedience, communion, worship, and praise. The man or woman without the inner witness or indwelling of the Holy Spirit will not be able to understand and discern the things of God, because it is the Holy Spirit that gives a believer such understanding.

The man with out the Spirit does not accept the things that come from the Spirit of God, for they are foolishness to him, and he cannot understand them, because they are spiritually discerned (1 Corinthians 2:14).

The Holy Spirit of God is your personal teacher and He brings the word of God, the way of God and the will of God alive into your heart. It is a perceivable evidence of salvation for believers.

Examine yourselves to see whether you are in the faith....
(2 Corinthians 13:5a)

God wants you to have assurance of your salvation. But such assurance can only be based on the truth of His Word. Anything less will not pass the test. As I said at the beginning of this chapter, I had not wanted to really spend a lot of time on these basic components of Christianity. I felt like most Christians knew these things, but loud in my heart God said, "No they don't." He made it known to me that some would find freedom in chapter three. That right here in this chapter— false salvation would be exposed. True salvation according to the word of God would be revealed to many for the first time.

Many "Christians" are in bondage because they are not really "Christians" at all. They bought into a cheap salvation that cost them nothing. They have not truly surrendered their lives to Jesus. Their lifestyles are not much different than in their "pre-salvation" days. They experience defeat on a regular basis and depend on themselves and worldly methods much more than God. Their names are on an earthy church roll, but not the heavenly one. They have no inner witness of the Spirit and live by a standard they have set. Right is right according to what they believe, and they often measure themselves against the standards of the world instead of the standards of God.

I have been such a person as I shared with you in my testimony in this chapter. I sat in church for 20 years believing I was saved. I had no *personal* relationship with the Lord and no evidence of salvation and yet I believed I was saved. Well, you know the saying, "being in church does not make you a Christian any more than being in a garage makes you a car." We laugh at the saying, but many have staked their lives on "membership" not "relationship."

Several years ago, God gave me a vision, a spiritual picture, if you will. It was a picture of a sanctuary, perhaps any sanctuary on a Sunday morning. I looked and saw people everywhere. In the vision God told me to close my eyes then open them again. I did. When I opened my eyes for the second time, some of the people were no longer people, but billows of fire. They were sitting in church believing they were saved and yet they were really bound for destruction. God said, *"Somebody ought to yell fire!"* People were on fire everywhere. False salvation exposed and yet no one sounded the alarm. God's truth as revealed in His Word exposes such false salvation. His Word is His fire alarm. His Word is the only true test of salvation. Examine yourself. *It's a matter of life or death.*

"Examine yourselves to see whether you are in the faith. Test yourselves. Do you not realize that Christ Jesus is in you – unless of course you fail the test?"
(2 Corinthians 13:5)

Chapter 4

Out of Egypt

It isn't that they can't see the solution;
it is that they can't see the problem.
-G.K.Chesterson

For every true believer in Jesus Christ, salvation is the road out of Egypt. Even though our salvation experiences may be drastically different, the road out is not. There is only one way and Jesus is the way. When you get "saved", God will lead you, by His Son, out of a lifestyle of sin no matter how strong or subtle the bondage may have been and no matter how young or old you may be. Biblically, "Egypt" has been a metaphor for "worldliness", sin city, if you will. Our Egypt represents a place of entrapment. For the Israelites, Egypt once looked good. It was the place flowing with grain and commerce. Out of their lack and during a time of famine, the Israelites went to Egypt. They enjoyed the riches and pleasure of Egypt and then became trapped them. They found themselves ensnared in Egypt—captive literally by harsh slave masters and a way of life that offered no hope, no joy and no way out. We are not much different. We too, are lured by desires of fortune, fame and fantasy. We will run to our Egypt to feed our pride, our greed, our lust, our stomach, our eyes, and anything within us hungry. We too, eat out of the wrong grain vats and become bound by that which we desired. For many of us captivity has become our way of life. But through salvation provided by Jesus Christ, our Deliverer speaks to the Pharaoh, the task master of our sin, and says, **"Let my people go."** It was a command of God then, it is still a command of God today!

Moses spoke the bold words under the unction and the direction

of God Himself. This Word of God is still out there, still command-
ing release for every bound up child of God. This Word of God, the
Bible says, will not return to God until it has accomplished the
purpose for which He spoke it (Isaiah 55:11). The purpose? —
freedom. Moses' ministry was a fore-shadow of the ministry of
Jesus Christ. Moses was the deliver of the first generation to come
out of Egypt; Jesus would be the Deliverer for *every* generation.
Moses revealed the need, Jesus met the need. It would be the hope
of deliverance that would be offered for every generation to come.
The exodus from Egypt was symbolic of, not only leaving physically, but leaving spiritually the surroundings and practices of
ungodliness. It would take trust, obedience, and perseverance to
leave Egypt.

Leaving Egypt

As Moses prepared the people to leave, very explicit instructions were given to each household. Such instruction would be
extremely important and have significance for this generation and
every generation that would follow. Each household was to take a
male lamb without defect and slaughter it at twilight (Exodus 12:5).
They were then to take some of the blood of the lamb and put it on
the tops of the doorframes of their houses. That same night they
were to get dressed and be ready to leave, then roast and eat the
lamb. They were also to prepare bitter herbs and bread without
yeast. As night approached, they would then be ready to eat the
food and depart in haste, as the Egyptians would beg them to leave.
It was on this night that God would deliver the final plague on
Egypt. He would send a destroying angel throughout the land of
Egypt to strike dead every firstborn – both men and animals
(Exodus 12:12). For the Israelites to escape the "death angel" it
would require obedience to the commands and instructions God
had given to them through Moses. When the destroyer went through
the land, he would *pass over* the homes that had the blood sprinkled
on them. Thus, by the blood of the lamb, they would be spared
death. I think it's important to note here that God did not command
the sign of the blood because he couldn't distinguish between the

Egyptians and the Israelites. He commanded the sign of the blood as an act of obedience to His word and surrender to His plan of redemption. The whole Exodus is a picture of redemption, our redemption that would soon come through God's Lamb, Jesus Christ. For every generation, anyone so desiring to be "saved," "delivered," and "spared death," they too would also have to come out "under the blood." For every generation the same obedience and surrender to the blood of the Lamb would be required. For New Testament believers, God supplied the blood of the perfect Lamb without blemish that was required for *Passover*, salvation, deliverance—REDEMPTION! The Hebrew word *Passover* literally means "to spare".[1] Our "sacrificial lamb" is Jesus Christ and it is His blood that God requires to be over the doorframe of our hearts for us to be "spared" the destroying angel—death. Know this: God still looks for the blood! The blood is a sign of obedience and surrender to the command and will of God. The blood is still a sign for death to *pass over.* The blood of Jesus provided a "pass over" from eternal life for "whosoever believes" and acts in faith and obedience. Take note here, no one, *not even one*, would come out of "Egypt" except by the blood of the lamb. The death and blood of the Lamb would become the doorway for life and freedom.

Leaving the Yeast Out

The requirement of the eating of the lamb represented identification with the lamb's death. To *partake* was literally *to be part of* the death that saved them. Similarly, the taking of the Lord's Supper is the New Testament believers' way of identifying and being part of Christ's death for us. We do so in "remembrance" of Him – the giving of His life for ours. The Passover lamb was to be eaten along with unleavened bread, which is bread without yeast. Since yeast in the Bible symbolically represents sin and corruption (Exodus 13:7, Matt 16:6, Mark 8:15,) this unleavened bread would represent the "leaving out," the "separating" of the redeemed Israelites from Egypt (worldliness and sin). Similarly, all God's redeemed people are called to separate themselves from the sinful world and to dedicate themselves to God alone (i.e. to "leave the yeast out!"). Such separation was God's command then; it is also God's command now. Every redeemed child of God is held to the same standard.

A little yeast works through the whole batch of dough. (Galatians 5:9).

Religion that God our Father accepts as pure and faultless is this, to keep oneself from being polluted by the world (James 1:22).

As the Israelites prepared to leave Egypt, one of Moses' main tasks was to teach them what the Lord expected of them. They were to be a holy people separated from pagan immorality and idolatry of their surroundings. God's plan of redemption not only included deliverance, but separation – worldly separation. More important than God removing the Israelites physically from Egypt was to remove them spiritually. The Bible tells us that even though *we are in* this world we are not to be *of* this world (John 17:14, John 15:19), nor are we to *love* the things of this world.

Do not love the world or anything in the world. If anyone loves the world, the love of the Father is not in Him. For everything in the world – the cravings of sinful man, the lust of the eyes and the boasting of what he has and does – comes not from the Father, but from the world (1 John 2:15-16).

... Do you not know that friendship with the world is hatred toward God? (James 4:4)

Such a friendship with the world may be why so many of us have so much trouble getting out of Egypt. Loving the world and the "things" of the world more than God, has long been a source of entanglement for God's children. Such love or friendship with the world, and the things of this world, has been defined as spiritual adultery— that is unfaithfulness to God and our commitment to Him. It involves embracing the world's ways, values, and pleasures, however innocent they may seem. Oh, we would never say that we do this, but often our actions and lifestyles confirm it. Noted Christian author, James Dobson, uses this quote, *"What you do speaks so loudly, I can't hear what you are saying."* We can say all day long we are Christians, we love God, we love Jesus, but our actions may prove differently. God has defined in His Word what loving Him looks like in behavior, thought, and deed. He also makes it clear what "not loving Him" looks like too! He said friendship with the world is as hatred toward Him.

What *is* friendship with the world? "Friendship" as defined by my 1828 Noah Webster dictionary is "mutual attachment, intimacy". It is this mutual attachment, this affectionate loving pursuit of titles, status, money, people, places, pleasures, etc., that God identifies as the culprit of faithfulness to Him. It is when we set our affections on such things that we will seek after, go after and pursue them, other than God. Such *affection* breeds a love for this world and the things of this world. Such love causes one to be devoted to the values, morals, interests, ways and pleasures associated with the "things" we sought. It's a package deal so to speak. Such a pursuit is what is so offensive to God. Our God is a jealous God and He does not love us with a divided heart nor does He desire love from us out of a divided heart. The Bible says, **"No one can serve two masters. Either he will hate the one and love the other, or he will be devoted to the one and despise the other"** **(Matthew 6:24).** Jesus spoke these words concerning mainly the love of money, but the *divided condition of the heart* was the essence of the exhortation. Division creates unfaithfulness. Unfaithfulness is sin before God. Let's look again at James 4:4-6, this time out of *The Message* translation.

You're cheating on God. If all you want is your own way, flirting with the world every chance you get, you end up enemies of God and his way. And do you suppose God doesn't care? The proverb has it that "he's a fiercely jealous lover" and what he gives in love is far better than anything else you'll find.

God desires faithfulness and it is for this reason He calls us to separate from the very things that cause unfaithfulness—the hindering, ensnaring, things of this world. Every spiritual journey out of Egypt begins with "laying aside," that is separating from, the things that "have so easily entangled us" (Hebrews 12:1). According to 2 John 2:16 quoted above, "things" that entangle can be divided into three categories: "The cravings of sinful man," "the lust of the eyes" and "the boasting of what he has and does." Let's explore each.

The Cravings of Sinful Man

"The cravings of sinful man" include impure desires and running after sinful pleasures and sensual gratification. The King James Version translates it as "lust of the flesh." Our flesh is our natural or sinful nature with corrupt desires. Lust of the flesh is an inordinate, immoral eager desire to please the corrupt nature. One of the corrupt desires is sexual immorality.

As the author, I would like to insert a personal note before we go any further. One, I use the term author very loosely, because my reality is one of a "scribe." I believe with all my heart I am just writing out the message of God's heart for His church. The paragraphs that follow would perhaps have been left out of "my" book. I struggled including such graphic definitions of the topic at hand. Again, in my mind I debated with God that most everyone knows the definition of sexual immortality, impurity, etc. He reminds me once again His purpose for this book coming forth is because His church is in bondage because "they do not know truth or do not apply truth." Every time we get to a section such as this, I wrestle with, "We know this," He counters with, "No you don't." The truth is we live in a world where even the leadership of our nation debated the definition of what sex is. The media, a host of journalists and every broadcast outlet known to man, had an opinion of the boundaries and definitions of sex. Each debating the other, to determine the morality of a president – that some would use as their moral compass. But let's be clear right here – God is not vague, nor is His Word, when it comes to sex, morality, or immorality and the likes. It is for this reason, that I believe God desires such graphic definitions to be included. Each definition is supported by scripture. For the church to walk free from bondage of sin, we need our reality to be based on truth. Our morality is to be based on truth. The only absolute truth is the Word of God.

Sexual immorality and impurity, as Biblically defined, includes not only forbidden intercourse or consummated acts, but also involves any act of sexual gratification with another person other than one's marriage partner, achieved by uncovering or exploring the nakedness of that person. [2] God's standard explicitly prohibits having any kind of "sexual relations with" (literally "uncovering the nakedness of") anyone who is not a lawful wife or husband (Leviticus 18:6-30, 20:11, 17, 19-21). Biblical terms used for sexual immorality describing the breadth of its evil, are as follows:

a. **Sexual immorality** (Greek: *porneia*) describes a variety of sexual activities before or outside of marriage; it is not limited to consummated sexual acts. Any intimate sexual activity or play outside the marriage relationship, including the touching of intimate parts of the body or seeing another person's nakedness, is included in this term and clearly transgresses God's moral standard for His people. [3]

b. **Debauchery or sensuality** (Greek: *aselgeia*) denotes the absence of clear moral principals, especially disregard of sexual self-control that maintains pure behavior, the opposite of which would be modesty. It includes the inclination toward indulging in or arousing sinful lust (desire) and thus is a participation in Biblically unjustifiable conduct[4] (Galatians 5:19, Ephesians 4:19, 1 Peter 4:3, 2 Peter 2:2, 15).

c. **Exploiting** or taking advantage of someone (Greek: *pleonekteo*) means to deprive another of the moral purity that God desires for that person in order to satisfy one's own self-centered desires. To arouse in another person sexual desires that cannot be righteously fulfilled is to exploit or take advantage of that person[5] (1 Thessalonians 4:6, Ephesians 4:19).

d. **Lust** (Greek: *epithumia*) is having an immoral desire that one would fulfill if given the opportunity (Ephesians 4:19, 22; 1 Peter 4:3; 2 Peter 2:11; Matthew 5:28).

Sexual immorality is particularly offensive to God. More than any other sinful act it "violates the sacredness of our own bodies; bodies that were made for God-given and God-modeled love for 'becoming one' with another." I like the way *The Message* translation words the particular scriptures concerning this.

There's more to sex than mere skin on skin. Sex is as much spiritual mystery as physical fact. As written in Scripture, "The two become one." Since we want to become spiritually one with the Master, we must not pursue the kind of sex that avoids commitment and intimacy, leaving us lonelier than ever—the kind of sex that can never "become one." There is a sense in which sexual sins are different from all others. In sexual sin we violate the sacredness of our own bodies, these bodies that were made for God-given and God-modeled love, for "becoming one" with another. Or didn't you realize that your body is a sacred place, the place of the Holy Spirit? Don't you see that you can't live however you please; squandering what God paid such a high price for? The physical part of you is not some piece of property belonging to the spiritual part of you. God owns the whole works. So let people see God through your body (1Corinthians 6:18-20; *The Message*).

"Sex is not just skin to skin." Sex has a spiritual facet as much a physical facet. Sex involves oneness, or becoming one with another. Sex involves commitment and intimacy according to God's standard. Sexual immorality bypasses the spiritual to get to the physical to feed a corrupt desire. Sexual immorality transgresses God's design and desire for sexual intimacy. Sexual immorality is an operation of "the cravings of our sinful man" or the sin nature of man. Other cravings are found in Galatians 5:19-21.

The acts of the sinful nature are obvious: sexual immorality, impurity and debauchery; idolatry and witchcraft, hatred,

discord, jealousy, fits of rage, selfish ambition, dissensions, factions and the like. I (Paul) warn you, as I did before, that those who live like this will not inherit the kingdom of God.

Those who live like *this*, Paul says, will not inherit the kingdom of God. Let's define "this" as listed in the scripture above.

1. **Sexual immorality**– already covered in previous paragraphs
2. **Impurity -** (Greek: *akatharsia*), i.e., sexual sins, evil deeds, and vices, including thoughts and desires of the heart [7] (Ephesians 5:3, Colossians 3:5).
3. **Debauchery -** (Greek *aselgeia*), i.e., sensuality; following one's passions and desires to the point of having no shame or public decency [8] (2 Corinthians 12:21).
4. **Idolatry -** (Greek: *eidolotria*), i.e., worship of spirits, persons or graven images; trust in any person, institution or things as having equal or greater authority than God and His word [9] (Colossians 3:5).
5. **Witchcraft -** (Greek: *pharmakeia*), i.e., sorcery, spiritism, black magic, worship of demons and use of drugs to produce "spiritual" experiences [10] (Exodus 7:11, 8:18; Revelation 9:21, 18:23).
6. **Hatred -** (Greek: *echtru*), i.e., intense, hostile intentions and acts; extreme dislike or enmity [11] (Leviticus 19:17; 1 John 2:9, 4:20; Proverbs 10:12).
7. **Discord -** (Greek: *eris*), i.e., quarreling, antagonism; a struggle for superiority [12] (Romans 1:29, 1 Corinthians 1:11, 3:3).
8. **Jealousy -** (Greek: *zelos*), i.e., resentfulness, envy of another's success [13] (Romans 13:13).
9. **Fits of rage -** (Greek: *thumos*), i.e., explosive anger that flamed into violent words or deed [14] (Colossians 3:8)
10. **Selfish ambition -** (Greek: *eritheia*), i.e., seeking of power[15] (2 Corinthians 12:20, Philippians 2:3, 1 Peter 5:5, James 3:14-16).
11. **Dissensions -** (Greek *dichostasie*), i.e., divisive teachings not supported by God's Word [16] (Romans 13:13, 16:17;

Galatians 1:9; Proverbs 6:16-19, 16:28, 28:25, 29:16).

12. **Factions** - (Greek: *hairesis*), i.e., divisions within the congregation into selfish groups or cliques that destroy the unity of the church [17] (2 Corinthians 12:20, Titus 3:9-11).

13. **Envy** - (Greek: *phthonos*), i.e., resentful dislike of another person who has something that one desires [18] (Proverbs 14:30, Mark 7:20-23, 1 Corinthians 13:4, James 3:14).

14. **Drunkenness** - (Greek: *methe*), i.e. impairing ones mental or physical control by alcoholic drink [19] (Proverbs 23:21; Ephesians 5:14; Romans13:12-13; 1 Corinthians 6:10; 1 Peter 4:3-4).

15. **Orgies** - (Greek: *komos*), i.e., excessive feasting and revelry, a party spirit involving alcohol, drugs, sex or the like [20] (Romans 13:12-13, 1 Peter 4:3).

Such definitions establish truth that perhaps the church has denied or avoided for quite some time. We don't like our definitions quite so "*defined.*" Vagueness begets ignorance and ignorance begets excuses or justifications. Perhaps the church dodges such truth, as graphic as it might be, so we can justify doing some things we are doing and still be "Christian." The Bible makes it clear only foolish people think they can compromise the Word and ways of God and live a Christ-centered life. The Bible does not support such thinking. The *sin of compromise* has invaded the church's mentality and stolen the freedom that life in Christ offers. Compromise is rooted in self-centered needs. It is our selfish nature that prefers reinterpreting God's commands to please ourselves. But compromise leads to destruction. Compromise was the sin that brought tragedy to Lot's family. In Genesis 18 and 19, the Lord revealed to Abraham His plans to destroy the cities of Sodom and Gomorrah where Abraham's nephew Lot, had chosen to live. Sodom and Gomorrah were cities filled with wickedness, and such wickedness had reached the heart of God (Genesis 18:20). Abraham had given Lot his choice of land and Lot chose the more fertile well-watered site near Sodom. Lot failed to take into account the wickedness of the city and instead chose "to pitch his tent toward Sodom" (Genesis 13:12) Although Lot was distressed by the filthy deeds he saw and heard (2 Peter 2:7-8); he still was willing to tolerate the wickedness of Sodom for the social and material advantages. [21] This compromise brought tragedy to his family. Through Abraham's plea God sent angels in the form of men to warn Lot and his family of God's impending plan. Upon hearing the news, his daughters fiancé laughed and shrugged it off as a joke (Genesis 19:14). The angels urged Lot to hurry and take his daughters and his wife out of the city. When they hesitated, the men grasped their hands and led them out with only one instruction. "Flee for your lives! Don't look back and don't stop anywhere in the plains." (Genesis 19:17) But Lot's wife did not take the Lord's word seriously. She looked back and was struck dead.

But Lot's wife looked back and she became a pillar of salt (Genesis 18:26).

Sodom and Gomorrah were destroyed. Lot lost his wife and two future sons-in-law because he tolerated wickedness in order to get what he wanted. Such a lifestyle had consumed his wife. She died looking back, clinging to the pleasures of Sodom. Such *compromise* cost her, her life. Jesus warns believers to "remember Lot's wife" (Luke 17:32) meaning that those whose hearts are attached to the world's corrupt values and pleasures will not be spared. The tragic error of Lot's wife was to place her "affections" on earthly things instead of heavenly. She turned back because her heart was still in Sodom. [22] It was friendship with the world, which is always a deadly compromise. The *sin of compromise* wreaked devastating consequences on Lot. Even after Lot fled Sodom and had encamped at a place called Zoar, his own children began to mimic the behavior they had witnessed all those years in Sodom. The Bible records that his own two daughters enticed him to drunkenness and then to incest. The ungodly behavior of the Sodomites, tolerated by their father all those years, had caused them to adopt such low moral standards for their lives. Because of Lot's compromise he lost his family and even his descendants became pagans. [23] It was the "sinful cravings of man" that caused Lot's wife to yield. Compromise will not conquer sinful behavior. Instead compromise becomes a noose around our neck that hangs us in "our Sodom."

The Lust of the Eyes

The second behavior of worldliness is "the lust of the eyes" (1 John 2:15-16). It's the immoral desire to have what I see. It refers to coveting or lusting after things that are attractive to the eyes but forbidden by God. It was such behavior that consumed Eve and caused God to banish her from the garden of His presence (Discussed in Chapter 2). She wanted what she *saw,* even though it was forbidden by God. David fell into the same entrapment when he *saw* Bathsheba bathing on the rooftop. (2 Samuel 11:2). He "coveted" what he *saw.* Coveting involves the desire or lust for all that is wrong or belongs to another person. [24] Coveting brings such destruction that God set it as the 10th commandment.

You shall not *covet* your neighbor's house. You shall not covet your neighbor's wife, or his man servant or maid servant, his ox or his donkey, or anything that belongs to your neighbor (Exodus 20:17; emphasis mine).

Coveting is fed by what the eyes see and desire. Paul sums it up this way:

Indeed I would not have known what sin was except through the law. For I would not have known what coveting really was if the law had not said, "Do not covet" (Romans 7:7).

But let's also read the very next verse.

But sin, seizing the opportunity...produced in me every kind of covetous desire (Romans 7:8).

Our human nature with its corrupt desire constantly looks for an outlet to express itself. Any door of opportunity will do. A quick glance can turn into a downward spiral that leads to painful consequences within one's life. Just ask David. The lust of his eyes led to

adultery, then to murder and then to the death of his own son (2 Samuel 12:15-18). Most assuredly sin has a progression. Sin will seize the moment! Paul further explained in this way.

"I know that God's commands are spiritual, but I'm not. Isn't this also your experience? Yes. I'm full of myself – after all. I've spent a long time in sin's prison" (Romans 7:14-16; *The Message***).**

Isn't that the truth! Sin's prison has held a lot of rebels. Those who did not take care, or precaution of what the eyes saw. It is part of our corrupt nature that has great potential to destroy.

Sin seizing the opportunity...deceived me, and through the commandments put me to death (Romans 7:11).

It's the very reason Jesus went so far to say that one should gouge out the eye if it causes one to sin or to lust (Matthew 5:27-28) . His reasoning – **"It is better for you to lose one part of your body than for your whole body to go to hell."** Enough said.

The Boasting of What He Has and Does

The third identified worldly behavior is the "boasting of what he has and does" (1 John 2:15-16). Boasting means "to speak with pride, vanity or exaltation with a view to self-commendation." [25] In other words, it is to magnify or exalt self. It is the "tooting of one's own horn," so to speak. As *The Message* translation puts it, it is **"being full of your grandiose self"** (James 4:16). This scripture further states, that all such "boasting is evil." The root cause of such behavior is *spiritual arrogance*. Boasting is based on the false assumption that whatever we accomplished, we did by ourselves and not with the help of God and others. It reeks of self-sufficient independence that does not recognize God as Lord. It is manifested by a spirit that seeks to exalt, glorify and promote oneself as the center. [26] Through the prophet Jeremiah, God addressed the issue of boasting.

This is what the Lord says: "Let not the wise man boast of his wisdom or the strong man boast of his strength or the rich man boast of his riches, but let him who boasts boast about this: that he understands and knows Me, that I am the Lord, who exercises kindness, justice, and righteousness on earth, for in these I delight" (Jeremiah 9:23-24).

Any and all boasting allowed has been pared down to one category – our relationship with the Lord. No other boasting is accepted in the sight of the Lord. All worldly knowledge, human ability or earthy riches pale in significance when compared to a knowledge and relationship with God.

Some boast in chariots and some in horses, but we boast in name of the Lord our God (Psalm 20:7; *New American Standard*).

No king is saved by the size of his army; no warriors escapes by his great strength. A horse is a vain hope for deliverance; despite all its great strength it cannot save. But the eyes of the Lord are on those who fear him, on those whose hope (boast) is in his unfailing love to deliver them from death and keep them alive during famine (Psalm 33:16-19).

Only one boasts counts – the Lord's.

Let him who boasts boast in the Lord. For it is not the one who commands himself who is approved but the one the Lord commands (2 Corinthians 10:17-18).

Know this: What you say about yourself means nothing in God's kingdom. It's what God says about you that counts. God deals with spiritual arrogance. His Word says **"For whoever exalts himself will be humbled" (Matthew 23:12).** In other words, **"If you walk around with your nose up in the air, you're going to end up flat on your face" (Luke 14:11 *The Message*).** The opposite of spiritual arrogance is humility. God will humiliate the one who boasts "in what he has and what he does." Boasting is a behavior detestable to the Lord. It's an entrapment that comes from the worldly lure to "be somebody." Jesus defines being a "somebody" this way: **"the greatest among you will be your servant" (Matthew 22:11)**. It's the upside-down gospel that we better get right-side up, lest such prideful thinking claims our minds and our actions. Let's be clear. It's not what we have or what we do – it's who we know!

Practically everything that goes on in the world – wanting your own way, wanting everything for yourself, wanting to appear important – has *nothing* to do with the Father. It just isolates you from Him (1 John 2:17; *The Message*).

Every spiritual journey out of Egypt begins with "the laying aside of everything that hinders and the sin that so easily entangles" (Hebrews 12:1). Flirting with the world and the ways of the world is dangerous. Such flirting opens the door to lifestyles and behaviors that "cheat on God."

And do you suppose God doesn't care? The proverb has it that "He's a fiercely jealous lover." And what he gives in love is far better than anything else you'll find (James 4:5-6a; *The Message*).

"Leaving the yeast out" was not an insignificant detail then or now. It is the last instruction before exiting Egypt. The partaking of the Lamb and the bread without yeast are details that cannot be overlooked. To follow God *out* of Egypt we must follow *in* obedience. Partial obedience *is still* disobedience. In essence, God was saying leave the "sin" behind. What you have "partaken of" in Egypt has no place on this journey – leave it out! *Separation is essential!* Walking out of Egypt begins by walking away from our sin and the worldliness we once enjoyed. It is an act of obedience that God will not waiver. Such an exit out of Egypt demands obedience to the instruction. As the old hymn says "Trust and obey, for there's no other way to be happy in Jesus, but to trust and obey."[27]

81

But if you do not drive out the inhabitants of the land, those you allow to remain will become barbs in your eyes and thorns in your sides. They will give you trouble in the land where you live (Numbers 33:55).

Chapter 5

I Obviously Need Help

For if I know the law but still can't keep it, and if the power
of sin within me keeps sabotaging my best intentions, I
obviously need help!
Romans 7:17 (*The Message*).

I know that God's commands are spiritual, but I'm not. Isn't this also your experience? Yes. I'm full of myself – after all, I've spent a long time in sin's prison. What I don't understand about myself is that I decide one way, but then I act another, doing things I absolutely despise. So if I can't be trusted to figure out what is best for me and then do it, it becomes obvious that God's command is necessary.

But I need something more! For if I know the law but still can't keep it, and if the power of sin within me keeps sabotaging my best intentions, I *obviously* need help! I realize that I don't have what it takes. I can will it, but I can't do it. I decide to do good, but I don't really do it; I decide not to do bad, but then I do it anyway. My decisions, such as they are, don't result in actions. Something has gone wrong deep within me and gets the better of me every time. *It happens so regularly that it's predictable.* The moment I decide to do good, sin is there to trip me up. I truly delight in God's commands, but it's pretty obvious that not all of me joins in that delight. Parts of me covertly rebels, and just when I least expect it, they take charge. I've tried everything and nothing helps. I'm at the end of my rope. Is there no one who can do anything for me? (Romans 7:14-24; The Message, emphasis mine)

Has Paul been reading your mail? Mine too! He makes some

great observations. One is that he realized, like we all must, that *knowing* God's commands is not enough to keep us from sin. Secondly, sin has power – sabotaging, entrapping and destructive, power. Thirdly, Paul recognized a repetition to sin. He seemed to trip up in the same places. He would decide to do right and yet each time end up doing wrong. It was predictable! He also realized the active rebellion within his own soul – all parts were not on the same page! The New International Version translates Paul's summation this way, **"What a wretched man I am." (Romans 7:24)**. It is the state of us all – absence of Jesus! But for the blood bought, redeemed, set free, child of God, this is not the case. We are no longer slaves to sin, but set free to walk away from sin by the provisions of Jesus.

...Through Christ Jesus the law of the Spirit of life *set me free* **from the law of sin and death. For what the law was powerless to do in that it was weakened by the sinful nature,** *God did* **by sending his own Son in the likeness of sinful man to be a sin offering. And so he condemned sin in sinful man (Romans 8:2-3; emphasis mine).**

The "law of the Spirit of Life" is the regulating and activating power and life of the Holy Spirit operating in the hearts of believers.[1] It is the power of God that sets a "believer free." The Holy Spirit comes into sinners and frees them from the power of sin that Paul and all of us are familiar with. Such power allows each believer to overcome sin. The "law of sin and death" is the controlling power of sin, which places people in bondage and reduces them to "wretchedness." Many of the statistics today show very little difference between the divorce rates among believers as compared to non-believers. There is also little difference in the percentages of those who struggle with addictions to pornography and alcohol among the two groups. So what's wrong? Why are so many Christians struggling with sin? Why is the church in bondage if indeed the Son has set her free? Why isn't the church looking a lot differently, at least statistically, from the non-believers who are entrapped and being held in bondage? What is the problem? Could it be application of truth, or actually, the absence of application of truth? Could it be that in the church, believers are not applying truth – truth that sets us free? Such truth begins with the knowledge that every believer has the power to overcome sin. No one has to be overcome, overwhelmed, trapped or caught up in sin's control. This power is the Holy Spirit of God inside every believer. When God says **"Come out and be separate"** (2 Corinthians 6:19), He also provides the means to do so – such means is His Holy Spirit. If we have the Holy Spirit, the very power of God, then what is the problem? Answer... the Holy Spirit doesn't have us! In order for the Holy Spirit to work effectively in the life of the believer, the believer must surrender or yield control to the Spirit.

So I say, live by the Spirit, and you will not gratify the desires of the sinful nature. For the sinful nature desires what is contrary to the Spirit and the Spirit what is contrary to the sinful nature. They are in conflict with each other, so that you do not do what you want. But if you are led by the Spirit, you are not under the law (Galatians 5:16-18).

Living by the Spirit and being led by the Spirit are keys to overcoming bondage and experiencing the freedom Jesus has provided for believers. But the Holy Spirit cannot lead if you are! The lead "dog," so to speak, has to be determined. Who's in charge has to be decided. If we are, Galatians makes it clear what we might expect. Under our leadership, sooner or later our sinful inclinations will take control, because there is no greater force to stop them. Such inclinations were listed and defined in Chapter Four of this book. Paul made a stern and forceful statement when he said,

Those who live according to the sinful nature have their minds set on what that nature desires; but those who live in accordance with the Spirit have their minds set on what the Spirit desire (Romans 8:5).

We can speculate, based on the statistics, that an unnecessarily large percentage of the church is NOT living in accordance with the Spirit. To "live in accordance with the Spirit" is to surrender, submit and yield to the Holy Spirit's direction and enablement, and to concentrate one's attention on the things of God. [2] *It is impossible to follow the sinful nature and the Spirit at the same time, because they don't lead the same direction.* One leads toward God, the other away. Surrender to the Spirit is the key to "living by the Spirit" or "being led by the Spirit." Surrender means *"to yield to the power of another."* The "another" for Christians is God through his Son Jesus Christ, led by the Holy Spirit. There are three parts to our surrender. As Christians, we must surrender to the will of God, the way of God, and the word of God. True surrender cannot yield to the will of God without yielding to the way of God; nor can we yield to Word of God without yielding to the will of God. For example, true surrender is not taking His word and walking it out *our* way. Why? Because His ways are not our ways! His ways are higher (Isaiah 55:8-9). The Christian faith is based on a life surrendered to Jesus Christ. Our lives include our actions, behaviors, thoughts, words, and more. We are called as Christians to take the higher path, morally, and spiritually and to live Godly lives that reflect Jesus. The Bible says, **"His divine power has given us *everything* we need for life and godliness (2 Peter 1:3; emphasis mine).** The provision for a godly life has been deposited within us. We are without excuse. The crux of the matter really comes down to one thing – surrender! Jesus said, "I am the way," He did not say *you* are the way! There is no other way to righteousness, right living before God, than the path the Spirit leads. Let me share three very practical ways of "living by the Spirit." They are summed up in three words: *yield, wait, and receive.*

Yielding

If you are truly a Christian, the Holy Spirit of God will operate in your life through internal warnings, impressions and nudges. As we mature in our walk with Christ, we will become more sensitive to the Spirit and actually recognize such promptings more quickly. But even at the onset of our Christian lives they are there. Sometimes my heart feels like it is pounding when the Holy Spirit is trying to get my attention. Other times it is like a flashing light internally that reads "danger." Years ago a popular television program "Lost in Space" had a robot that always seem to appear at just the right time to alert the space crew of impending danger. He would come out of nowhere with his repetitious alert "Warning, Warning, Warning." The space crew had the same choice you and I have. We can heed or resist. The Holy Spirit is *our* internal warning system! Sometimes the Holy Spirit alerts me in a very quiet voice. It's like hearing a word or instruction very faintly. It often causes me to pause just to be able to hear— but I hear, and so do you. It's the gift of God for every believer. The Bible makes the role of the Holy Spirit in our lives very clear. The Holy Spirit:

- *reveals to us the truth about Jesus.* "But when He, the Spirit of truth, comes, He will guide you into all truth" (John 16:13; See also John 14:16, 21; 16:13).
- *convicts us of guilt.* "When He (Holy Spirit) comes, He will convict the world of guilt in regard to sin and righteousness and judgment" (John 16:7-8).
- *gives us new birth in Jesus Christ.* "I tell you the truth, no one can enter the kingdom of God unless he is born of water and the Spirit. Flesh gives birth to flesh, but the Spirit gives birth to Spirit" (John 3:5-6).
- *He is our divine teacher.* "But the Counselor, the Holy Spirit, which the Father will send in My name, will teach you all things and remind you of everything I have said to you" (John 14:26;See also John 16:13, 14:26; 1 Corinthians 2:9-16).
- *sanctifies us, cleanses us, lead and motivates us to live holy lives.* "But we ought always to thank God for you... because from the beginning God chose you to be saved through the sanctifying Word, the Spirit, and through belief in the truth" (2 Thessalonians 2:13; See also Romans 8:24; Galatians 5:16-17; 2 Thessalonians 2:13).
- *empowers us for service.* "And you shall receive power when the Holy Spirit comes on you and you shall be My witnesses..." (Acts 1:8).
- *gives us spiritual gifts to edify or strength the church.*

"Now to each one the manifestation of the Spirit is given for the common good." "All these (gifts) are the work of one and the same spirit, and He gives them (gifts) to each one just as He determines" (1 Corinthians 12:7,11).
- *promotes righteousness.* (See John 16:8 above; see also 1 Corinthians 3:16).

The list of the work of the Holy Spirit is long. It includes all those listed above and more such as, enables us to proclaim God's word (Acts 1:8, 4:31), builds the church (Ephesians 2:22), inspires worship (Philippians 13:3), helps us in our prayer life (Romans 8:26-27), produces Christ-like character that glorifies Jesus (Galatians 5:22-23; 1 Peter 1:2), imparts God's love to us (Romans 5:5), gives us comfort, joy, and help (John 14:16; 1 Thessalonians 1:6).

Church we have EVERYTHING we need pertaining to life and godliness by the divine power and presence of the Holy Spirit. *The problem is not having what we need – the problem is not using what we have!* Think about this, the power of God (we're talking God Almighty here!) is available to you and I in every circumstance and situation of our lives. It is available to enable us to walk free of sin. The Holy Spirit is God's provision to us so that we can be all He has destined us to be. It is not up to us. It never has been! It's the work of the Holy Spirit. Our part comes down to one action – surrender, that is yielding to the Spirit. I won't make light of the gravity of that action because it takes a tremendous amount of trust to yield to the power of another. But for Christians, it's not optional *if* we are going to follow Christ and become Christ-like. The Spirit knows the way, the will, and the word of God. He also knows how to use all three to transform us, set us free, enable us and empower us to be all that God has determined for each of us in His kingdom.

Waiting

When we surrender to the Holy Spirit, we are then required to wait. This action is not even found in the "to do" list of many. The word wait has been treated like a "curse" word in many circles. Perhaps it's because the meaning has been so misinterpreted.

Biblically, "waiting" is a "determined stillness." It is a determined stillness designed to cause you to pause until you receive further instruction or guidance. Waiting does not mean doing nothing. Waiting is a time of listening. Waiting also requires trust. We must trust God's timing to deliver what we are waiting for. If we don't trust Him and His timing, waiting will only create anxiousness. There are some Biblical directions tied to our waiting such as, **"Be still and wait patiently for him" (Psalm 37:7).** Another translation says, **"Be still and rest in the Lord; wait for him patiently" (Psalm 37:7; *Amplified Bible*).** Wait? Patiently? That goes against every human fiber of our being doesn't it? Most likely. But waiting is a tool in the hand of God that helps spare us from hasty wrong decisions. Waiting helps us hear so we can heed the direction of the Lord. A rule around our house is "when in doubt, don't." Most of us know how to blast past the Holy Spirit's signals. It's right up there with running red lights and rolling through the stop signs. But refusing to wait, to be still, can be costly. Refusing to wait can usurp the timing of God.

The heart of the matter is again trust. Waiting and trusting are inseparable – ask Abraham. His name was actually still Abram at this point but for ease of text we will use his God given name. Ishmael, Abraham's first son was born because Abraham and his wife Sarah wouldn't wait on the promise of God. God had promised that Sarah and Abraham would have a son even in their old age (Genesis 15:2-5). When it didn't happen in the time frame they thought, Sarah encouraged Abraham to bear a son with their maidservant. They no longer trusted that God was going to do what He said. The maidservant bore a son and the name given him was Ishmael (Genesis 16:1-16) But God reminded Abraham of his promise to him and Sarah. Thirteen years later, Sarah bore the promised son and named him Isaac (Genesis 17:15-19).

Through the ages, Ishmael has come to represent the impatience of man and the product of human effort. Many of us birth "Ishmaels" because we will not wait. Impatience is an evil tool of Satan to get Christians to abort the plan and will of God. Impatience tempts us to human effort rather than relying on God's effort. Impatience most often creates a work of the flesh rather than a work of the Spirit! Ishmael is also a picture of distrust. Abraham and Sarah lacked trust that they would receive what God had promised. If you follow the genealogy of Abraham's descendants you will see that Ishmael became the father of today's current Arab nation, which is mainly located in Palestine. Isaac, the child of promise became the father of the Jewish nation known today as Israel. There has been a continuing war between the Arab nation (descendants of Ishmael) and Israel (descendants of Isaac). Even today there is much bloodshed. Such is often the case when presumption (rooted in impatience) runs ahead of promise (rooted in obedience). When we surrender and wait, the promise is this – we *shall receive*.

After Jesus' crucifixion and before His ascension He told His disciples to wait in Jerusalem. Waiting would be required for them to receive what God had for them. The direction and instruction for the operation of the Holy Spirit in our lives has not changed from the day Jesus spoke it into being. Surrender and waiting bring about the receiving.

Receiving

Receiving what? POWER.

Do not leave Jerusalem, but wait for the gift my Father promised, which you have here me speak about...but you will receive power when the Holy Spirit comes on you; and you will be my witnesses.... (Acts 1: 4, 8).

Such power is the *divine dynamic ability* of God for our lives. The word power in the Greek is "dunamis." It's where we get our word dynamite. It's God on the scene, a heavenly explosion of provision! It's more than strength or ability it is also authority – God given authority. It's the power and authority to put to death the misdeeds of the body. It's enablement to walk away from temptation. It's the strength and courage to overcome addictions, ungodly behavior, language and the likes. It is guidance for the right decisions and choices we need to make. It's our spiritual compass towards God. It's the unction of God to accomplish the will of God in the life of every believer. It's our witness of God to a watching unbelieving world! It begins with surrender –that is appropriated in our lives by waiting and is manifested (seen) by receiving. Philippians 2:3 says, **"For it is God, who works in you to will and to act according to His good purpose."** Jesus taught the disciples about receiving in John 15:5. He said,

I am the vine; you are the branches. If a man remains in me and I in him; he will bear much fruit; apart from me you can do nothing.

This is a truth that must be embraced if we are ever going to walk victoriously. "Apart" from Jesus, our human effort will fail. God never created us to succeed independently apart from Him. It was not His plan in the beginning; it is not His plan now. He makes these things clear in this scripture. *Provision flows to the branch from the vine*. He is the vine. We, as the branches, are to *receive* the provision. To put it another way, we are "sap suckers." Every branch on a tree receives nourishment (i.e. sap) from the "vine" or "tree" That's the source for the branch's life. The branch doesn't have to produce the sap; it just has to *receive* it. The sap in the branches then produces fruit. The branch didn't produce the fruit. It will however "bear" the fruit. To "bear" simply means to carry. The fruit was produced from the sap that flowed to the branch from the vine. Are you getting the picture here? Our sap, if you will, is the provision, power and authority of God that flows in the life of every believer in the form of the Holy Spirit. The sap (Holy Spirit power) produces godly fruit in the life of a believer. Such fruit as: love, joy, peace, patience, kindness, goodness, faithfulness, gentleness, and self-control (Galatians 5:22-23) is a product of the Holy Spirit. We didn't produce it. The Holy Spirit (sap) produced it within us. This Holy Spirit- produced fruit is the virtue of God working in us to convert us to "Christ-likeness."

It is the help we obviously need! It's the "something more" Paul said he needed. It's the conquering force of God that overcomes, overwhelms and overtakes the enemy of our souls. It's the counter-attack to our rebellion. Listen again to the truth of God. He said, **I**

have given you everything pertaining to life and godliness (2 Peter 1:3).

Church we are not power-less, we are powerful, power-filled people! We have what it takes to walk in the manner pleasing to our God. It is realized in our life when we surrender, and yield control to the Holy Spirit. Surrender is a discipline. The more we do it the better we will get at it, because we will begin to see the benefit associated with surrender. The benefit is "receiving" what we need. Some could argue it's not in the not knowing, it's in the not doing. Know this: God even supplies what it takes to surrender. He is familiar with our weakness to yield control. However He says, **"My grace is sufficient for you, for my power is made perfect in weakness" (2 Corinthians 12:9).** *The Message* translation says it this way, **"My grace is enough; it's all you need. My strength comes into it's own in your weakness."** Declare your weakness before God. It's okay to do that. God's grace is His presence, His power, and His favor. For the believer, it's a force, a heavenly strength, for all those who call on God. Perhaps you have not because you ask not. (James 4:2). Surrender and the strength to surrender, comes by asking then yielding. God will supply when we ask (Philippians 4:19). It is a provision of God that cannot be matched anywhere else. It will take practice, practice, practice, on the part of every believer to live the surrendered life. Proverbs 5:23 tells us that a man will die for the lack of discipline. Such a discipline of surrender is key to living by the Spirit.

"Live by the Spirit and you will not gratify the desires of the sinful nature" (Galatians 5:16).

Chapter 6

A Leap of Faith

Faith means believing in advance what will only
make sense in retrospect
-Phillip Yancey

A Leap of Faith

To live the surrendered life involves trust – trust in God. Trust in God is the foundation of faith in God. **You cannot have faith in someone you do not trust**!

One night as a man was walking along a path, he stumbled over a cliff and fell a considerable distance before catching himself on a branch, which had a small piece of rope attached. Looking down, he realized that he might be killed if he dropped to the ground, and there seemed to be no way to climb back up. So he began yelling for help.

"Is anybody there?" he yelled. As soon as he yelled out a calm voice answered back, "Yes, I am here."

"Who are you?"

The voice responded, "I am God."

After another pause, the man asked, "Can you help me?"

God answered, "Yes."

The man then replied, "What do you want me to do?"

God answered, "Let go of the limb and depend on me to save you."

This time there was an even longer pause. Finally, the man called out again, "Is there anybody else up there?"

Funny story, uh? We chuckle, but we don't really like God's answer do we? Let go of the rope? It was the most secure thing the man had. Exactly! God was asking him to let go of that which gave him the greatest sense of security. He trusted the rope more than he trusted God. Sound familiar? Like the man hanging on the branch, some of us "are hanging" in our life circumstances, too.

We often feel there is no one who can help us. Sometimes our circumstances evolve to where we think it is hopeless. We often look for help to come in a certain way and when it does not match our expectations *or* requires more than we are willing to give well… we just hang. We hang on what *we think* is security. We hang instead of letting go and letting God. We hang instead of letting go and letting God catch us, provide for us, help us, save us! The real issue for the man at the end of the rope was TRUST – TRUST IN GOD. In his circumstances, he yelled out for help. God answered… not the way he thought and not even the way he wanted. His response to God proved that he did not trust God. What about us? Ever been at the end of your rope? Perhaps some of you reading this book right now are "dangling." Some may even feel they are "hanging hopelessly." Perhaps feelings of helplessness, isolation, and loneliness have also made their way into your mind, your emotions, and even your heart. Some of you may have circumstances that seem impossible – that seem to have no real answer.

Several years ago when I was still a working mom, I found myself hanging at the end of my rope. As a professional woman, and the head of a medical department in a training institution, I had received many awards and promotions for my work in my field. I had climbed the career ladder rapidly and had become part of a team (mostly physicians) in the work I was doing (obstetrical ultrasound and radiology). At this point in my life, my love and passion had become my work. I was having amazing success at detecting early fetal abnormalities to which aided the doctors in early intervention of pregnancies in distress. Most of my zeal and energy were given to my profession. Even though I was a career woman, I was also a mom. I had three small children – two of whom were twins! My morning routine consisted of getting three kids dressed, fed, and to daycare with diaper bags, lunches, and the likes, so I could arrive at the clinic before eight am with a clean, white, pressed uniform on. Often I would be well into my day before I realized what I had on! Everything was mechanical. Sometimes my day would go late depending on our patient load or emergency cases that might demand overtime. I would then have to scramble to find a "substitute mom" who would pick up my children. My husband's job demanded he travel a lot so his help was not always available. He was often gone several days at a time so juggling such a schedule took toll on our family, our marriage, and even my health. I loved my job however. It was the only place that I felt I received accolades. It was the only place that I felt I excelled. It was my *"security blanket."*

So imagine my surprise when I finally yelled for help and God gave an answer I, too, could not trust. The toll of the job, the schedule, the kids, and the stress had caused me to yell out. I screamed to God that I could not do "this" anymore. Everything in my life was falling apart – even me! I yelled loudly, "God help me!" He answered back, "Quit your job!" Now, for a lot of women that would have been a divine answer – but not for me. I LOVED my job. I did my job well. I got accolades and acceptance from my job. My employer had just bought me one of the finest pieces of ultrasound equipment anywhere around! Quit my job? Never! It was my sanity place.

The answer disturbed me even more, because it was the same one my husband had given me several months earlier. He wanted me to quit—to stay home—to be a stay at home mom! I didn't like the answer anymore from him than I did from God. So what did I do? Well……..I decided to just hang. I hung desperately for another whole year! The weight of hanging nearly destroyed my marriage, my family, and my health. One very restless night I went back to the clinic after hours. I sat in the darkness of my office and cried. The weight of "hanging" was too great. There that night I decided to let go and let God…… I decided to trust Him and that His answer was right. I decided to surrender my will to His. And so….. I let go.

God caught me and He immediately began working His plan into my life. Everyday became a TRUST DAY. As I adjusted to my new life at home, health returned to me, my family and my marriage. My prayer became, "O dear God, please make it be that I would never have to go back to work again!" I was enjoying immensely the new things God was doing in my life. **He** had become my security and my priority.

God has a plan for your life too. His word says **"He has a plan to prosper you and not to harm you, plans to give you hope and a future (Jeremiah 29:11).** This plan –*His plan*—is your destiny. It's the very reason God made YOU. It has to do with every part of you; where you work, live, who you marry, if you marry, who your friends are and so on.

So many people have no idea of God's design for their lives. So many have yet to really begin walking in their destiny because... well, because they won't let go and let God direct. Letting go involves trust—trust in God. Trust in God is the foundation of faith in God. YOU CANNOT HAVE FAITH IN SOMEONE YOU DO NOT TRUST! That bears repeating... **You cannot have faith in someone you do not trust**. Trust is the foundation of faith. I heard this poem in a tape I was listening to. I want to share it with you. It's entitled *Romans 8:28*.[1]

Romans 8:28

Listen little children, I'd like you all to know
Some things you might find helpful in times of care and woe
I never take a lunch break, nor will you see a sign
Back in 10 minutes – I'm sure you'll cope just fine.
I've never been caught napping, or slept since time begun
I've never needed 40 winks, Reread Psalm 1-2-1
I've never flown to Florida, Just desperate for a break
Nor left a deputy behind, I'm God for goodness sake!
So lift your eyes from trouble and trust me as you should
For I'm the one who works all things,
Together for your good!
Heather Cooke

Even now, while you are reading this book, God is not slumbering – but He is at work on your behalf, even now. Perhaps even now, God is whispering in your ear "Let go, let go. You can trust me. Let go."

God has a plan for your life so great that hanging on to a circumstance, a fear, an attitude, or even a relationship, could be stealing the *joy of walking in your personal destiny with* God. It is said that people hang on the "proverbial rope" for at least three reasons: *Fear of falling, Fear of failing, o*r the *Fear of feeling rejected.*

The **fear of falling** is most often experienced when you do something to embarrass yourself, humiliate yourself, something that makes you look like a fool. Whether it's true or not, you are sure everyone else's opinion of you has *fallen* as a result. You feel crummy, cruddy, and lonely inside, isolated by what seems to be your own stupidity. A fear of falling, deals with our *perceptions* of self, which are often conjured up scenarios in our mind.

The **fear of failing** shows up when we think we don't measure up – not to our own expectations – or even the expectations of others. You may feel you have failed to make the grade, make the team, or make the promotion. You may feel you've failed to be a real friend or even to win the love of someone special. Perhaps you feel you've failed your parents, or a spouse, or even God, by something you did or said. As a result you feel disappointed in yourself, guilty, and alone and you don't know how to fix it. A fear of failing, deals with *perceptions* of self based on past experiences and disappointments.

The **fear of feeling rejected** is one of the most widely shared fears and it comes when we are not accepted by our peers at any age. We may feel rejected when we are not included, overlooked, or when someone doesn't respond the way we had hoped. Perhaps we have been rejected because we are different, because of our convictions, or for no reason that we understand. As a result, we often feel alone. The fear of feeling rejected, deals with *perceptions* of self based on others reactions to us.

The *fears of falling, failing, and feeling rejected* cause us to cling even tighter to our "rope." Such fears can cause "us" to depend on "us" even more. It seems too risky to trust others and it seems even riskier to trust God so… we just hang. Hanging can soon create a feeling of helplessness and even hopelessness. So what can we do? Find truth! We can find truth about our circumstance because the Bible says, "**You shall know the truth and the truth shall set you free" (John 8:32).**

God's people are bound up everywhere, because they do not know His truth or they do not apply His truth to their own situation. This whole book is about knowing and applying truth. Truth leads to freedom! Let me share some truth with you a moment.

Truth from Isaiah 41:10 —**So do not fear, for I am with you; do not be dismayed for I am your God and I will strengthen you and help you; I will uphold you with my righteous right hand.** It's truth!

Truth from Isaiah 40:29, 31— **He gives strength to the weary and increases the power of the weak... but those who hope in the Lord will renew their strength. They will soar on wings like eagles; they will run and not grow weary, they will walk and not faint.** It's the truth!

Truth from Hebrews 13:5b—...**God has said, 'Never will I leave you; never will I forsake you" So we say with confidence, "The Lord is my helper; I will not be afraid. What can man do to me?"** It's the truth!

Truth from Psalm 46:1—**God is our refuge and strength, a very present help in times of trouble.** It's the truth!

And lastly, although I could go on forever!

Truth from Isaiah 30:20-21— **Although the Lord gives you the bread of adversity and the water of affliction, your teachers will be hidden no more; with your own eyes you will see them. Whether you turn to the right or to the left your ears will hear a voice behind you, saying, "This is the way; walk in it."**

It's the truth! It's the truth that God **is** trustworthy! Don't say you have faith in God, if you don't trust God *because you cannot have faith in someone you do not trust*! Trust is the foundation of faith. God *is* trustworthy – His ways *are* trustworthy. His word, His will, and His ways hold the plan and promises for your life. Plans and promises that will catch you every time you let go! Faith means trust. Trust means letting go. And letting go means letting God show you the best way, the "high" way, the right way for your life!

Let me tell you two stories – one from Hollywood and the other from the Bible. First one up – Hollywood. It's an unlikely place to find a parable – a story with spiritual implications – but I found it while watching the movie, "The Karate Kid."[2]

The Karate Kid

It's a very old movie but the message stays fresh – even today. In an effort, to learn to defend himself, Danny, the lead character, decides to take karate. By a series of circumstances and some begging he gets one of the great karate teachers, Mr. Miyagi, to agree to teach him. Danny is perplexed when he shows up at Mr. Miyagi's house for his first lesson and the great instructor informs him he must sand his floor. After a rebellious fit and a trip home, Danny finally agrees, thinking the teacher is taking advantage of his youthful energy. As Danny sands, Mr. Miyagi corrects his techniques and demands he uses certain strokes and go in certain directions. Danny is furious and lets Mr. Miyagi know that he came for karate not sanding. Mr. Miyagi doesn't budge much to Danny's surprise.

Lesson number two doesn't go any better. Upon returning to Mr. Miyagi's home, Mr. Miyagi hands Danny a paint brush and instructs him that today's lesson is to paint the fence and the house. "No way," Danny declares. After another fit and another trip home, Danny finally surrenders to the paint job and incorporates the precision brush strokes the great instructor demands.

With the painting all done Danny is now ready for Karate 101. Instead, Mr. Miyagi takes Danny out back of his home and shows him his fine car collection. Danny is in awe of the prestigious old cars in mint condition. Mr. Miyagi even lets Danny sit in his favorite choice. Danny imagines himself in such a car, but soon reality snaps in and Danny reminds Mr. Miyagi of the lesson. Mr. Miyagi agrees and throws Danny car wax and a wax cloth. He begins to show Danny how to wax the cars. By this time Danny has had it and pronounces once again in immense frustration, "I'm here for karate!" Mr. Miyagi simply says "Yes, I know," and proceeds with the waxing instructions.

Once again under protest Danny leaves. What is wrong with this man he wonders? Sulky and pouting, Danny wanders back, more out of curiosity than anything else. Desperate to get the karate lesson, Danny succumbs to the old instructor demands. Once again, he begins to wax furiously when the strong hand of Mr. Miyagi stops the rampant pace and replaces it with a gentle and precise skill. Mr. Miyagi shows him two movements – wax on and wax off. He coaxes Danny to do the motions. More perplexed than ever, Danny caves to the verbal instructions, "Wax on, Wax off!" Day in and day out, all the cars were polished with the two simple motions.

Upon completion of the task, Danny pleads for the lesson. Mr. Miyagi agrees. Skeptical, Danny awaits his first position of karate. To his surprise Mr. Miyagi calls out a familiar instruction, "Sand the floor." "What?" "Sand the floor." As Danny is ready to bolt, Mr. Miyagi mimics the position, the simple motion he had required of Danny. Little had Danny known that the movement of sanding the floor was a foundational move of karate. The days and weeks it took to sand the floor, to paint the fence and the house had built Danny's muscle and instilled the correct karate moves into his memory. Little did Danny know that "sand the floor," "paint the fence," "paint the house," "wax on – wax off" were all the basic components of karate moves. Little did Danny know that everything the great instructor had required of him that had "seemed" so useless, were the very things he needed to know to excel in karate. Danny misread and mistrusted the instructor's demands. He had no idea that everything he was doing was to accomplish the very thing he desired. Sound familiar?

His ways are not our ways but *His ways always accomplish His purposes.* Sometimes, we too, misread and mistrust His ways. We refuse to "sand the floor" and "wax" the cars. We let the rope dangle instead of grabbing hold. We are so sure "this" has nothing to do with "that" that we, too, rebel, walk away, or walk past the very things God intends to use to build faith and trust and release His promises in us. Faith is trusting His ways, *even when we don't understand*!

Get your feet wet

My second story is found in Joshua 3:1-17. The entire Israelites nation is standing at the banks of the Jordan River ready to cross over to the Promised Land. Only one problem: the Jordan is at flood stage. The orders had already been given, **"When you see the ark of the covenant of the Lord your God, and the priests, who are Levites, carrying it, you are to move out from your positions and follow it"** (Joshua 3:3). All eyes were on the priest. What would they do? Joshua, the leader of the Israelites, told the people, **"Consecrate yourselves, for tomorrow the Lord will do amazing things among you"** (Joshua 3:5). The people prepared. Even Joshua must have wondered how they were going to cross. Perhaps he was alone at the waters edge, when the Lord spoke to him and said,

"Today I will begin to exalt you in the eyes of all Israel, so they may know that I am with you as I was with Moses. Tell the priests who carry the Ark of the Covenant: 'When you reach the edge of the Jordan's waters, *go and stand in the river*' " **(Joshua 3:7-8; emphasis mine).**

That doesn't seem too difficult does it? Not really except… the Jordan is at flood stage and did I mention the banks of the Jordan River go straight down. When you step in – you're in; if you know what I mean! The Lord further explained to Joshua, **"As soon as the priests who carry the ark of the Lord – the Law of all the earth – set foot in the Jordan, its waters flowing downstream will be cut off and stand in a heap"** (Joshua 3:13).

Good news, right? Sort of. You see what God basically told Joshua was that nothing will happen until you *take a leap of faith* and get your feet wet. That's right – feet! *Both in!* Before anything happens both feet must be in! I did mention that the banks go straight down and the river is at flood stage, didn't I? Joshua knew this, so did the priests. They knew that when the priests stepped in they were going to either be in over their heads or God would do as He said and the river would divide. It took faith in God to make such a bold move. Faith that He would do what he said He would do. But the priests would only know by getting their feet wet. *Nothing would happen until they stepped in.*

Ever been there? You know between the rock and the hard place? Ever had your back against the proverbial wall? Ever been at a crisis of belief – the kind where if God doesn't show up you die? Maybe emotionally, maybe mentally, maybe even physically! My human nature wants God to divide the river first and then I'll walk through. But that takes no faith and God desires to build faith in His children. He does so by circumstances that require trust. A *leap of faith* is always the first step towards God. We come to God and into the Promised Land by faith! By Leaps!

If the priests of Israel had not had faith in God – placed their trust in God, well... the whole nation of Israel might still be standing on the other side today! You know what I'm saying? Often we fail to experience the goodness of God, the deliverance of God, the promise of God, because we won't take the leap – let go – get our feet wet. Such obedience, such trust, such faith unleashes a power of God that you won't know until you step in! Joshua 3:15-17 records the results:

As soon as the priests who carried the ark reached the Jordan and their *feet* touched the water's edge, the water from upstream stopped flowing. It piled up in a heap a great distance away. While the water flowing down to the Sea of the Arabah was completely cut off, the priests who carried the ark of the covenant of the Lord *stood firm on dry ground in the middle of the Jordan*, while all Israel passed by until the whole nation had completed the crossing on dry ground" (Emphasis mine).

Nothing happened until they stepped in! In order to step in they had to completely trust that God was a man of His word! Their *leap of faith* unleashed a power of God that led them into the promises of God, but it all required faith and a leap! Faith means trust. Trust means taking the leap, letting go and letting God show you the best way, the "high" way, the right way. Taking the leap gets you from where you are to where God desires you to be – the Promised Land.

My oldest child has graduated from college and my twins have just left for college. My nest is now empty, but I am not. Over these past 16 years since quitting work, since "letting go," I have had numerous opportunities to be a servant for the Lord in my own family and with others. Upon quitting my job, God immediately sent teachers into my life to mentor me and teach me His truths. He then entrusted me to teach these same truths to others. For seven years, I had the privilege of starting and teaching a Bible memory program at my local church. I got to help kids (even my own!) memorize and learn the Bible. It is a program that is still being used at our church today. After that, a door opened for me to lead a Bible study for adults in my church. Soon another door opened to serve as chaplain to a local college women's basketball team. It has been a joy and a delight to mentor these young women. Every opportunity has brought me closer and more dependent on God than I could ever have known. In 2002 God allowed me to be the "birth mother" for a prayer center in our city. To date, this has been my greatest venture, although writing this book may rival the experience!

My point for telling you all this – is this. If I had not let go of my rope – I would have hung there (been suspended in time) and missed God's desire, design, and destiny for my life. I've got a question for you. What are you hanging on to? What has become your security rope? I've got a better question for you. Are you willing to let go and let God? It's just a question.

O Sovereign Lord, you are God! Your words are trustworthy, and you have promised good things to your servant (2 Samuel 7:21).

Trust in the Lord with all your heart and lean not on your own understanding; in all your ways acknowledge Him, and He will direct your paths (Proverbs 3:5-6).

Chapter 7

The Setting of the Soul

He (Moses) was in the assembly in the desert with the
angel who spoke to him on Mount Sinai, and with our
fathers; and he received living words to pass on to us. But
our fathers refused to obey him. Instead, they rejected him
and *their hearts turned back to Egypt*
Acts 7:38-39 (emphasis mine)

The Setting of the Soul

The children of Israel had made it out of Egypt. God had miraculously parted the Red Sea. They had safely passed to the other side. They were definitely on their way to the Promised Land. Things seemed to be going well until… until about the third month. The entire nation of Israel was assembled in the desert at the base of Mt. Sinai. God had called Moses to come up the mountain to meet with Him to give Him the law for the people. It would be His rules for holy living, His will for the people's behavior (Exodus 19 and 20). The Israelites would be expected to obey the laws so that they could live in a blessed relationship with God (Deuteronomy 28:1-2, 30:15-20). While Moses was on the mountain, a party broke out at the base, an unexpected party of sorts. You see, it had been a bad day at the base. The kids were fighting; some marriages were really being strained from all the travel and constant change. Some couples weren't even speaking! The money pouch was out of balance (whose fault was that?) and the food… well let's just say … it was no McDonald's out there! The murmuring and complaining was getting louder. Something had to give. Each needed comfort, relief, release – something! They were tired of waiting on God; they were tired of waiting on Moses. They turned…. **"They turned their hearts back toward Egypt."**

He (Moses) was in the assembly in the desert with the angel who spoke to him on Mt. Sinai, and with our fathers, and he (Moses) received living words to pass on to us. But our fathers refused to obey him. Instead, they rejected him and in their hearts turned back toward Egypt (Acts 7:38-39).

In their discomfort, discontent and disbelief, they disobeyed God. Rather than revere Him they rebelled against Him. They turned back to the old, the familiar. They turned back to the ways of Egypt. Old and familiar has its place, but not when it comes to sinful behavior. The turning of the heart was loud and obvious and it took on the shape of a golden calf.

When the people saw that Moses was so long in coming down from the mountain, they gathered around Aaron and said, "Come, make us gods who will go before us.
As for this fellow Moses who brought us up out of Egypt, we don't know what has happened to him" (Exodus 32:1).

So they all took off their gold jewelry gave it to Aaron and he made it into a "seeable" god (Exodus 32:3 *The Message*).

He (Aaron) took what they handed him and made it into an idol cast in the shape of a calf, fashioning it with a tool (Exodus 32:4).

Golden Calves

Golden calves. We all have had them. Look in your closet. Look in your driveway. Look in your checkbook. Counterfeit security measures — the "seeable." Things and possessions; the "something" that will give comfort, give relief, make you happy, take away your misery— some "thing". Counterfeit salve— Counterfeit trust— Counterfeit dependence.

The Israelites looked no different than the world they had just left. They indulged in eating and drinking and revelry. There was boisterous activity and sexual promiscuity. It was a party that by modern day standards would have attracted an "all networks'" coverage. Peter Jennings would have been there to interview Aaron. Tom Brokaw would have reported from the site of the calf. Dan Rather would have gotten Moses' first impression as he descended from the mountain. CNN would be first on the scene with live coverage. It was newsworthy and it did not fail to attract attention— God's attention. The sound of the party had reached His ears, and it released an anger in Him that scared even Moses (Deuteronomy 9:19).

Then the Lord said to Moses, "Go down because your people, whom you brought up out of Egypt, have become corrupt" (Exodus 32:7).

My people? What's up with that? Those aren't *my* people. Those are *your* people God. Can't you just hear Moses' thoughts? God continued.

"They have been quick to turn away from what I commanded them and have made themselves an idol cast in the shape of a calf"(Exodus 32:8a).

God may be in the heaven, but He knows everything that is going on- on Earth. He can detect a golden calf a million miles away and He was not happy.

They have bowed down to it and sacrificed to it and have said, "There are your gods, O Israel, who brought you up out of Egypt." "I have seen those people," the Lord said to Moses, "and they are a stiff-necked people. Now leave Me alone so that My anger may burn against them and that I may destroy them" (Exodus 32:8b-10).

Destroy them? Whoa! Moses' brain is now in overdrive. He's got a million plus people in the desert partying and making sport of God. They are about to get a holy zapping and don't even know it.

Moses pleads for the people before God.

Turn from your fierce anger; relent and do not bring disaster on your people (Exodus 32:12b).

Out of His love for Moses God relents. Moses heads down the mountain with God's law in his hands. No one notices, but the tablets are already broken... in spirit. Moses arrives on the scene. The camera pans close. The party's so loud they missed his entrance. He sees the calf and the people dancing around it. His anger burns. Camera 1 has him in full view, when all of the sudden, he throws the tablets to the ground. Camera 2 goes in for a close up. The tablets, who would have thought two pieces of stone, could make such a loud noise? But the anger gets worse.

And he (Moses) took the calf they had made and burned it in the fire; then he ground it to powder, scattered it on the water and made the Israelites drink it (Exodus: 32:20).

Talk about bitter water, this drink was especially hard to swallow. Moses had calmed God; now who could calm Moses? Moses turned his attention to Aaron. His own brother had fashioned the calf! "What is wrong with our family tree?" he must have thought. He said to Aaron, **"What did these people do to you, that you led them into such sin?"** Aaron is quick on his feet. **"Do not be angry my Lord,"** Aaron answered. Too late! **"You know how prone these people are to evil" (Exodus 32:22).** No truer words had been spoken. The Bible verifies that since the banishment from the garden, man has been rebellious and sinful, indeed prone to evil. In the New Testament, Paul called it "our history" and gave a warning.

"Remember our history friends, and be warned. All our ancestors were led by the providential cloud and taken miraculously through the Sea. They went through the waters in a baptism like ours, as Moses led them from enslaving death to salvation life. They all ate and drank identical food and drink, meals provided only by God. They drank from the Rock, God's fountain for

them that stayed with them wherever they were. And the Rock was Christ. But just experiencing God's wonder and grace didn't seem to mean much— most of them were defeated by temptation during the hard times in the desert and God was not pleased" (1Corinthians 10:1-5; *The Message*).

Let's push pause a moment on this "Crisis in the Desert." This is the "baptized," redeemed children of God, we're talking about here. Freed from Egypt and delivered from bondage. They had seen God's presence in the form of a cloud miraculously, leading them. They had seen the Red Sea miraculously parted for them. They were divinely sustained in the desert and had experienced God's amazing grace in the Exodus, and yet the Bible records most of them were defeated by temptation and died in the desert. What happened? Good question. Push "Play."

The same thing could happen to us. We must be on guard so that we never get caught up in *wanting, our way* as they did." And we *must not turn our religion into a circus* as they did. "First the people partied, and then they threw a dance." We must *not be sexually promiscuous*. They paid for that; remember with 23,000 deaths in one day! We must *never get Christ to serve us* instead of our serving Him; they tried it, and God launched an epidemic of poisonous snakes. We *must be careful not to stir up discontent*; discontent destroyed them (1 Corinthians 10:6-10; *The Message* emphasis mine).

What happened was that selfishness and rebellion took over. Push "Pause" again. Paul pointed out the downfall of the church in the wilderness. He identified five rebellious behaviors that lead to their demise.

1. Wanted their own way (i.e., set their hearts on evil things; selfish).
2. Turned their religion into a circus (i.e., pagan revelry, NIV calls it idolatry).
3. Participated in sexual promiscuity (immoral sex).
4. Wanted God to serve them; rather than they serving God

(tested the Lord).

5. Engulfed and destroyed by a discontent spirit (i.e., grumbling, murmuring, complaining, and dissatisfied).

These are hallmark behaviors of the Church (which includes you and me) that turn its heart back towards Egypt. Paul is making the point to the New Testament Church that God did not tolerate Israel's idolatry, sin, and immorality; and He will not tolerate ours either. The New Covenant in Christ makes payment for our sin, gives us forgiveness of our sins through the blood of Jesus, but *never tolerates* our sin. The New Covenant does not make way for believers to do as they please.

Our freedom in Jesus Christ does not make us free to do *whatever*. We are called to a higher standard. It is the same standard He set for the Israelites. A standard He required they obey. A standard He requires us to obey. Read on and take note.

These are all warnings, markers, DANGER, in our history books; written down so that we don't repeat their mistake. Our positions in the story are parallel- they are at the beginning- we at the end- and we are just as capable of messing it up as they were. Don't be so naïve and self confident. You're not exempt. You could fall flat on your face as easily as anyone else (1 Corinthians 10:11-12a; *The Message*).

Read the history book and learn! Did you hear that? Read the book and learn. Paul's point? — We are just as capable of messing up. We can either learn from their mistakes or we can repeat them. We are people prone (drawn) to do evil. We are not exempt from temptation and we are not excused from obedience. God set a standard. It's called the Law. The Law contains 10 commandments not 10 suggestions! Push Play and let's go on.

Back to the Mountain

The young intern got his first "field trip" to the base of Mt. Sinai that day. I don't remember if he was with Peter, Ted, or Dan, nevertheless, he came along for observation. He was curiously drawn to the crash site of the stones. As he reached to pick up one of the larger pieces another journalist approached. They both noticed that something had been written on the stones. Scrambling with the skill of a focused jigsaw puzzler, they worked to re-assemble the pieces. "What does it say?" the young intern inquired. "I'm not sure," the older more seasoned journalist replied. "Hand me another piece." When the last piece was put in place a hush came over the mountain. The stones began to speak.

"You shall have no other gods before Me" (No other gods, only me) **(Exodus 20:3).**

"You shall not make for yourself an idol in the form of anything in heaven above or the earth beneath or in the waters."(No carved gods of any size, shape or form of anything, whatsoever, whether they fly, or walk or swim.) **(Exodus 20:4).**

"You shall not take the name of the Lord your God in vain." (No using the name of God, your God, in curses or silly banter; God won't put up with irreverent use of His name.) **(Exodus 20:7).**

"Remember the Sabbath day to keep it holy." (Work six days and do everything you need to do. But the seventh day is a Sabbath to God, your God. Don't do any work…. For in six days God made Heaven, earth and sea, and everything in them; he rested on the seventh day. Therefore God blessed the Sabbath day; he set it apart as a holy day.) **(Exodus 20:8-11).**

"Honor your father and mother."(Regard, treat with honor, love, obedience and courtesy.) **(Exodus 20:12).**

"You shall not kill." (No murder) **(Exodus 20:13).**

"You shall not commit adultery." (Be faithful in marriage.) **(Exodus 20:14).**

"You shall not steal." (No stealing.) **(Exodus 20:15).**

"You shall not bear false witness against your neighbor." (Do not tell lies about others.) **(Exodus 20:16).**

"You shall not covet." (No lusting after your neighbor's house, or wife, or servant or maid, or ox or donkey. Don't set your heart on anything that is your neighbor's.) **(Exodus 20:17).**

Tablets of stone inscribed by the finger of God, with the Law of God (Exodus 31:18). The inscription had not even dried and yet the people's behavior was as broken as the stones upon the ground. What happened in the desert that day? Why were the people so quick to turn from God's commands? Why had they turned back to the ways of Egypt?

The New Testament gives us the answer, a diagnosis of that day, if you will. In the day of testing, of trial, of discontent, they fell back on the familiar. They turned back to their former ways, their old habits, rather than walking, waiting or persevering in the new ways of God. As Paul stated earlier, they wanted their own way. After all it is the path of least resistance and it IS familiar. We know such a path like we know the back of our own hand. It's "do-able." It's "comfortable." It's better than hanging around the base of the mountain, waiting on God, waiting on Moses, doing nothing.

Paul makes it clear that the Israelites *knew the word of God*, and *the will of God,* but they did not put it into practice. He had given His word to them personally through Moses and had written it on tablets of stone. Israel knew the will of God. After all He was delivering them out of Egypt and was taking them to the Promised Land. But Israel *did not know the **way** of God.*

...your fathers tested and tried me and for forty years saw what I did, that is why I was angry with that generation, and I said, "Their hearts are always going astray and they *have not known my ways*" (Hebrews 3:9-10 emphasis mine).

The "way" of God is obedience. He commands it on the route to freedom. It's His mode of transportation. Obedience transports us from Egypt to the Promised Land. Israel rebelled however and tested the Lord out in the desert. They got out of the car, so to speak. They threw a "hissy fit" and demanded their own way. Their "fit" transformed itself into a "me" party. Ever been to one of those? The wanting of their way was so strong they disregarded God to get it. But God will not be mocked nor made sport of. His ways are still His will whether we choose to practice them or not.

When I was in junior high and high school, I played basketball. I played for coaches that believed in year round practice. Our summers were filled with "two-a- days". We practiced at 7 a.m. and 7 p.m. daily. It seemed like we practiced a whole lot more than we actually played real games. About mid-summer the team would load up and go off to basketball camp for a week where we would play as many as five games per day. These games were practice situations so we could learn the right things to do to win in the games that did count. "We need to practice" was my coach's favorite line. We heard the same admonition over and over: Practice, practice, practice. Everyday he would give instruction and he expected us to put into practice what we heard.

Practice according to the dictionary means frequent or customary action; to perform certain acts frequently either for instruction, profit or amusement. It also means actual performance. Simply put, *practice is forming a habit of acting in a certain manner*. Most of us are very familiar with practice. The word alone conjures up thoughts of long hours at the piano; grueling rehearsals, continuous drills and endless repetition. Practice has become associated with pain and agony. We tend to avoid it at all cost. The discipline of practice however, is as old as the Bible. Jesus encouraged His followers to practice. He spoke about it this way.

Why do you call me, 'Lord, Lord,' and do not do what I say? I will show what he is like who comes to me and hears my words and puts them into *practice*. He is like a man building a house, who dug down deep and laid the foundation on rock. When a flood came, the torrent struck that house but could not shake it, because it was well built. But the one who hears my words and

***does not put them into practice* is like a man who built a house on the ground without a foundation. The moment the torrent struck that house, it collapsed and its destruction was complete (Luke 6:46-49 emphasis mine).**

Everyday Jesus was giving instruction to His followers. Foundational words of truth for life. He *expected* His followers *to practice* what they were hearing. He wasn't saying these things for His benefit but for theirs. If they were going to be "hearers" only He had a warning— a severe storm warning— with devastating consequences. Jesus said, **"In this world you will have troubles"** (John 16:33). Translation: Storms are going to come! Be they financial storms, emotional storms, relational storms, children or family storms, or job storms. Storms are going to come. Storms shake and during storms **"Everything that can be shaken will be shaken"** **(Hebrews 12:27)**. Only firm foundations will withstand the shaking in the day of the storms. The foundation is important. Every good builder knows the foundation determines the security and stability of the building.

My earthly father is a carpenter, a building contractor, as we call them nowadays. When he would get ready to start building a house, he would dig the foundation first. It was step number one and the most important step. My father would dig down until he hit the "hard pan." The hard pan is the solid, stable ground where he knew the foundation would not shift or sink. No blocks were laid until the hard pan was found.   Hearing and heeding the Word of God is the "hard pan" for every believer. It's step number one. God's truth and promises must be our foundation if we are to be solid, steady, steadfast, and immovable, Such a foundation is needed so we don't shift or sink when the hard times come. Jesus, the Master Carpenter, understands the devastation faulty foundations can cause. He was giving "building instructions" for every believer to follow. He knows the "building code" of a house that can't be shaken and won't crumble.

Firm foundations are built by *practicing* what we hear. God's building blocks will not help us unless they are put into place. On the hillside that day Jesus was speaking to His "team" and you know what He was saying? "Practice, Practice, Practice." There is no substitute for practice. It's foundational. It's key if you want to survive the storms of life. The Israelites missed it. They knew God, they knew His Word but *they did not practice His ways.* James 1:22 tells us, **"Do not merely listen to the word and so deceive yourselves. Do what it says!"** Listen to it again.

Don't fool yourself into thinking that you are a listener when you are anything but, letting the word go in one ear and out the other. Act on what you hear! Those who hear and don't act are like those who glance in the mirror, walk away, and few minutes later have no idea who they are, what they look like.
But whoever catches a glimpse of the revealed counsel of God— the free life!—even out of the corner of his eye, and sticks with it, is no distracted scatterbrain but a man or woman of action. That person will find delight and affirmation in the action. Anyone who sets himself up as "religious" by talking a good game is self-deceived. This kind of religion is hot air and only hot air (James 1:22-26; *The Message*).

The Christian life is walk, not just talk. It's hearing coupled with heeding. It's obedience by practice. It's how we shatter proof our lives. All storms are not caused by God, but all storms are allowed by God. Some storms are even sent as "building inspections" for our lives. Jesus knows what you have built your life upon. Such storms often reveal "rock" or "sand," so building corrections can be made. The Israelites did not put into practice what they heard and their lives fell apart like a faulty foundation. They knew God, they knew His will, but they did not practice His ways. They were defeated by temptation because "apart from God we can do nothing" (John 15:5). Sin causes us to be "apart."

According to scripture, **"Everyone who sins is a slave to sin"** (John 8:34). But through Jesus Christ, our slave status changed. If the Son has set you free, you are free, and no longer a slave to sin.

Don't you know that when you offer yourselves to someone to obey him as slaves, you are slaves to the one you obey- whether

**you are slave to sin, which leads to death, or to obedience which
leads to righteousness? But thanks be to God that, though you
used to be slaves to sin, you wholeheartedly, obeyed the form of
teaching to which you were entrusted. You have been set free
from sin and have become slaves to righteousness (Romans
6:16-18).**

Every born again, true believer in Jesus Christ has had their
slave status changed. We, who believe, were once slaves to sin,
under sin's control. Sin was our master. But now through Jesus
Christ, we have been set free. Looking back at the Israelites in the
wilderness, begs the question: "Is it possible having been set free, to
once again become a slave?" The answer— yes, it is possible.

**Formerly, when you did not know God, you were slaves to those
who by nature are not gods. But now that you know God, or
rather are known by God, how is it that you are *turning back* to
those weak and miserable principals? (Galatians 4:8-9).**

Paul was asking if we wished to be enslaved by our past sins all over
again. He was trying to warn the modern day Church that we are just
as capable of the same mistake as the Church in the wilderness.
Turning back seems to be a problem as old as the Exodus. *Turning
back* in essence, is to return to what you left—perhaps old behaviors,
attitudes, relationships, principals, or habits. *Turning back* is a
change of direction. It literally means to go backwards. To go backwards, as Christians, is to go back into slavery from freedom. How
does that happen? Answer—by returning to habits of our past.

**For if you live according to the sinful nature, you will die; but if
by the Spirit you put to death the misdeeds of the body, you will
live (Romans 8:13).**

Failure to put to death the misdeeds, "the sin habits" of the body
opens the back door to Egypt." If we do not participate with the
Spirit to kill our old nature, it will seek to rule us and once again
become our master.

It is for freedom that Christ has set us free. Stand firm, then, and do not let yourselves be burdened again by the voice of slavery (Galatians 5:1).

The insinuation here is that we have some responsibility in participating with the Spirit so that we do not once again get bound up by sin. Our responsibility is to apply (put into practice) what we have heard. Truth, God's truth, *applied*, will set us free and keep us free. The Israelites made the fatal mistake of *turning back* to former habits of their past. *Turning back* opens the access door to the enemy to come into our lives and get hold of us, a strong hold of us, in areas where we are weak. But our defense and guard is this,

You were taught with regard to your former way of life, to *put off your old self*, which is being corrupted by its deceitful desires; *to be made new in the attitude of your minds;* and *to put on the new self*, created to be like God in true righteousness and holiness (Ephesians 4:22-24; emphasis mine).

This scripture holds the prescription for "staying free". It is the prescription for living in the sustaining, enduring freedom provided for us through Jesus Christ. Take serious note here of what is being said. The prescription has three essential parts to *put into practice*— put off your old self; renew your mind; and put on the new self. It's Freedom Class 101. Get a notepad and let's get started.

#1 Put off your old self

Translation: Quit your old conduct.

One of the ways the church is in bondage today is failure to "put off the old self," that is, quitting the old conduct of our old life. When we come to Christ we must leave behind the ways of our past as we embark for the Promise Land. The journey for believers includes a process called *sanctification*. Sanctification is a big word with huge meaning. Sanctification means "to make holy, to consecrate, to set apart," as in separating from sin, so that we may have intimate fellowship with God.[1] Sanctification was God's will for the Israelites. They were to live holy and sanctified lives, separated from the lifestyles of the nations around them (Exodus 19:6). Sanctification is both a work of God *and* a work of His people. In order to accomplish God's will in sanctification, believers *must participate* in the Spirit's sanctifying work by ceasing to do evil.[2] In other words, "quit the old conduct." We often counter, "I would if I could." I've tried this line more than once myself, but it is not a truthful statement. God will not let us limp along behind this pitiful excuse. In 2 Peter 1:3 we are reminded that we have *everything* we need for life and to live a life of godliness. In 1 Corinthians 10:13 we are told that,

"There is no temptation that has seized us except that which is common to man. And God is faithful; he will not let you be tempted beyond what you can bear. But when you are tempted, he will also provide a way out so that we can stand up under it."

When we were saved, temptation did not cease, but we received "divine power" to overcome temptation. We received divine power to walk away, walk out, escape, resist, quit, lay aside, surrender, give up, put out, and put away our former way of life. And that's the truth; truth we *must apply*. Believers can no longer excuse away their behavior behind the excuse that they can't change, because every believer has the power within to change the behavior. It's the same power that raised Jesus from the dead. That's power! Such power operates in the believer's life through the Holy Spirit. Our responsibility is to cooperate with the Holy Spirit as He 'nudges" us and "impresses" upon us ways to clean up our house so to speak. As believers, we are temples of the living God. The heart is where Jesus resides. The Bible tells us in James 1:22,

"Get rid of all moral filth and the evil that is so prevalent and humbly accept the word planted in you, which can save you."

Moral filth...now who gets to define that? The Government? Society? The ACLU? Moral filth is defined in the Word of God.

God makes it clear what is acceptable and what is not. If you have trouble understanding or knowing if something is acceptable, get with a spiritually mature believer and ask them to help you sort this out. Moral filth includes, but is not limited to, obscenity through television, videos, movies, magazines, and language. It also includes sexual immorality as defined earlier in chapter four. It is drunkenness, debauchery, revelry and the likes (also discussed in chapter four). Believers are commanded to get rid of moral filth. "Get rid of" implies separation. Separation means.. .well, you know exactly what it means. It means "to sever, to part with, in almost any manner, things naturally or casually joined." Separation can be physical and spiritual. In either case, it's like sweeping out the house.

Years ago when I was first saved, I had an experience about the physical housecleaning of moral filth. I was rearranging a large bookshelf and sorting the books to put back when I ran across a book that had been given to my husband and me. It was a book written by a scientist that supposedly could predict the future and explain away our past, absent God, that is. As I held the book in my hand, the Holy Spirit spoke to me internally not audibly, "get the book out of your house." My heart pounded. I knew I was to throw the book away. Not only did it not honor God, it promoted thinking that was destructive. I promptly went to my kitchen and threw the book in the garbage can. Again the Holy Spirit spoke to me, "get the book out of the house." My kitchen was *still* in my house and He was impressing upon me to get it physically out of my house. I obeyed. I took the book in the trash bag and sat it on the curb for the garbage man to pick up. Now you may think that was extreme behavior, but I knew what God was doing. He was house cleaning my house of things that were not honoring of Him and things that were detrimental to His work in me or my family. I needed only to obey as the Holy Spirit led the way. I've repeated this process several times since then.

Anything in *your* house that might need to go? Now, I agree it is easier to just throw something out of our physical homes than it is our spiritual ones but the same procedure applies. The Word of God is the standard and the Holy Spirit is the "Merry Maid." Any behaviors, language, lifestyles, or moral filth has to go. Second Corinthians

6:17-7:1 tells us to "**Come out and be separate from the world, to purify ourselves from *everything* that contaminates body and spirit**" (emphasis mine). We do so out of obedience to God for the perfecting of holiness within us. Without holiness you will not see God (Hebrews 12:14).

My husband and I had the opportunity to take a Christian counseling course that was brought to our city. Our instructor, a well known and highly sought after counselor, gave a good example of what I am talking about.

He said a man came into his office who was a confessed alcoholic. It was his daily habit when he got off work to join up with some of his co-workers at a local bar. He would go by the bar to have a "few" drinks which would invariably turn into several. The habit had nearly destroyed his marriage and severely limited his work abilities. The man was now seeking counseling to change his ways. He told the counselor, "It is so hard. Everyday on my way home I still want to pull in to the bar. How can I change?" The counselor said, "Fellow, it's simple. Don't go by the bar!"

And God is faithful; He will always provide a way out of temptation. We may not like it. It may not seem reasonable to us, but remember God's ways are not our ways— His ways are higher. "Don't go by the bar" sounds too simple doesn't it? Maybe not. Quitting the old habits can be very difficult. Sometimes it takes *twenty-one times,* if you know what I mean (explanation later)! But as Christians we must create new habits into our life. Re-habituating our lives takes time. It takes *practice.* Remember practice? It's repeating certain acts frequently. Every temptation is an opportunity to do right. The old saying goes, "*As long as we have a chance to do right – do right.*" Practice is forming the habit of acting in a certain manner. You are not left on your own to do right. The Holy Spirit – the power of God residing in you— is your "enabler" to "not go by the bar." Call on Him; ask for the willpower, strength, courage, stamina, and steadfastness to do what is right.

Tony Miller, in an article written for *Charisma* magazine, summed it up this way, "God is big enough to change your weak-

nesses into strengths, your messes into ministries. He is not intimidated by your limitations. He already knows what they are, why they are, and where they are located." [3] The Lord stands ready to provide you with everything you need to walk free of your sin. It is yours for the asking.

#2 Renew your mind

Translation: Get a new attitude, a new mindset, a new way of thinking.

Webster's defines mind as "the understanding, the power that conceives, reasons, or judges inclinations, intentions, or purpose." Not only have we got to start acting differently, but we have to start thinking differently. Ephesians 5:26 says,

"...Christ loved the church and gave Himself up for her to make her holy, cleansing her by the washing with water through the Word."

The word of God is "Jesus soap." Its purpose is to clean up our worldly, stinkin' thinkin' as my friend, Brenda, puts it. Its purpose is to wash away mindsets and thoughts contrary to God. It's a reset button for where we have gone astray in our thoughts. Romans 12:2 says,

"Do not be conformed any longer to the pattern of this world, but be transformed by the renewing of your mind."

Renewing of the mind is essential for the transformation. The Bible says that **"as a man thinks in his heart, so he is" (Proverbs 23:7; *King James Version*)**. In other words, the head bone is connected to the heart bone! The "heart" in scripture is the totality of our intellect, our emotions, and our will. An impure heart will corrupt one's thinking, one's feelings, one's words and actions. A transformed heart transforms our thinking. [4] Our renewed or transformed thinking sustains for us the freedom Jesus provides for us.

Such transformation is key.

Jesus said, ...**"The things that come out of the mouth come from the heart and these things make a man 'unclean.' For out of the heart come evil thoughts, murder, adultery, sexual immorality, theft, false testimony, and slander" (Matthew 15:19).** Such "uncleanness" separates us from the fellowship and life in Christ. Every believer has to have the heart and mind renewed and transformed for freedom in Christ to be a present reality. Renewing of the heart and mind come by impartation and acceptance of the Word of God into ones life. Renewing involves a transition from an old life of sin to a new life of obedience. Scripturally, we are told to take every thought captive and to make it obedient to Christ. What does that mean? It means every time the old thoughts, the evil thoughts, the selfish thoughts, etc., come up, we need to immediately present them to God in prayer and ask Him to take them away. Did you know God can and will do that? Philippians 4:8 reminds us to think on whatever is true, noble, right, pure, lovely, admirable, excellent, or praiseworthy. It's the exchange of thought that will keep the mind pure.

If the mind is the battleground for the soul (and it is), then a Christian's warfare involves bringing all our thoughts into alignment with Christ's Word and His will. Failure to do so can lead to immorality and sin and ultimately spiritual death. When Christians refuse to bring their thinking (which affects their actions) into alignment it can cause a condition known biblically as "hardening of the heart." With every refusal the heart gets calloused and loses its sensitivity to God's work and the desires of the Holy Spirit. The Bible says,

"Today, if you hear His voice, do not harden your hearts, as you did in the rebellion, during the time of testing in the desert, where your fathers tested and tried Me for forty years and saw what I did" (Hebrews 3:8).

This scripture remind us of Israel's disobedicnce in the desert after their exodus from Egypt. It is a warning for New Testament believers. Because of the Israelites' failure to resist sin and remain loyal to God, most of them were barred from entering the Promised Land (Numbers 14:29-43). They hardened their hearts to the Word of God. If we ignore the voice of God through His written and inspired word, we run the same risk. Through the refusal to receive and be transformed by the Word of God, our heart, which interacts with our thinking, will grow increasingly hard and unyielding until it is no longer sensitive to God's Word or His Spirit. Such a loss of sensitivity is a great loss and can cause us to forfeit the freedom of the Promised Land. Such a loss can become a reality when believers fail to apply the truths of God to their lives. God's exhortations, warnings, promises, and teachings, must be heeded and implemented into the life of the believer for freedom in Christ to be realized. When the realities of the world become greater in the life of the believer than the realities of God, the believer can once again become a hostage, a slave, to the old life. Gradually, such a believer will cease to draw near to God. As they embrace the world and its ways, they no longer love righteousness and hate wickedness. Such behavior is a rejection of God's way that grieves the Holy Spirit in the soul of the believer (Ephesians 4:30, Hebrews 3:7-8, and 1 Thessalonians 5:19). So how do we have our minds renewed? By *reading and heeding* the word of God.

The word of God is dynamic and powerful and well able to accomplish such a work in each of our lives.

The word of God is living and active. Sharper than any two-edged sword, it penetrates even to dividing soul and spirit, joint and marrow; it judges the thoughts and attitudes of the heart (Hebrews 4:12).

The Word of God has power to cut away the old. It will examine our every motive spoken and not spoken. The Word of God is able to make hidden thoughts seen. Our reaction to the Word of God will determine our status of freedom. Believers are to eagerly hear God's Word and seek to understand it (Matthew 13:23). We must accept the Word of God and do what it says (Mark 4:20, Acts 2:41). We are to hide the Word of God deep in our hearts by reading and re-reading. We are to trust in it (Psalm 119:42) and live according to it (Psalm 119:9). *If you are not in the Word of God, there is a very good chance the Word of God is not in you!* Believers must establish the habit of being in the Word of God. This means reading, meditating, and praying the word. The Word of God releases grace, power and revelation by which believers grow in their faith and their commitment to Jesus Christ. The Word of God causes us to grow spiritually and is also our sword against Satan (Ephesians 6:17). Jesus defeated Satan in the wilderness by the Word of God (Luke 4:1-11).

Many years ago after becoming a new believer, I desired to establish the habit of getting up and spending time with God first thing every morning. I wanted to read, meditate and learn to pray the Word of God. A man in our couple's Bible study shared that he set his alarm to get up for his morning quiet time and treated the alarm as the Holy Spirit telling him to get out of bed. I decided to try the same.

My first morning was a total failure. My alarm went off. I got up and went into my designated "prayer chair" and promptly fell asleep! My second morning was like my first. I was devastated. I couldn't stay awake. I was ashamed to admit it—but not only could I not "tarry one hour" I could not tarry five minutes! I had two choices at this point. I could quit or keep trying. It was at this juncture that I vaguely remembered a scientific study that said anything you do *twenty-one times* in a row becomes a habit. Now, I don't really know if that's true or not but I set myself a goal to get up twenty-one times in a row. I prayed and asked God to help me stay awake each morning. Day number three I got up, stayed up, maybe five minutes before drifting back to sleep. The good news was— this was five more minutes than I had ever done! (small victory, but victory nonetheless!) My five minutes grew into ten, and my ten grew into fifteen. Eventually the fifteen turned to thirty and one day even thirty was not enough! I now enjoy a quiet time with God sometimes one to two hours before my day begins. A pastor friend of mine from New Zealand told me this. He said, "Discipline yourself. God will take the discipline and grow it into desire. He will then take the desire and grow it into delight." I can truly say that my morning time that began as a discipline is now a delight! I keep a quote in the back

of my Bible that keeps me motivated to get up and spending time
with God. It's by Pastor Charles Spurgeon and it says,

*"It is a good rule never to look into the face of man in the morn-
ing till you have looked into the face of God; and equally good rule,
always to have business with heaven before you have any business
on earth. Oh, it is a sweet thing to bathe in the morning in the love
of God"*

God's Word indeed washes us and cleanses us for the day at hand.
His Word establishes right thinking that leads the way to right
actions. It has been said that the godliness of our minds determines
to a large extent the godliness of our lives [6] The renewed mind
keeps a believer headed toward the Promised Land – the place of
God's presence, His provision and His protection.

#3 To put on the New Self"

Translation: Reset the soul

Everybody has a "past." Everybody. I've never met a person
who didn't have a "past." Our past most assuredly includes
mistakes, missteps and misdeeds we all regret. But Jesus said,
"Behold, I make all things new" (Revelations 21:5).

Every born again believer of Jesus Christ is a new creation. The
Bible says the old is gone, the new has come (2 Corinthians 5:17).
The new, is the person and presence of Jesus Christ residing in the
heart and life of the believer. The "new" transforms our past and
reshapes our present. "Putting on the new self" is instant at salvation, but the results are sometimes gradual. The new is not realized
by our fleshly human efforts, but by the Spirit. The Holy Spirit is
like your personal divine butler that holds out your "custom fit"
robe of righteousness" for you to put on. Alterations are made as
needed. Our righteousness is Jesus Christ. He is the only one who
can make us right with God.

...Clothe yourselves with Lord Jesus Christ, and do not think about how to gratify the desires of the sinful nature (Romans 13:14)

I delight myself in the Lord; my soul rejoices in my God. For he has clothed me with garments of salvation and arrayed me in a robe of righteousness (Isaiah 61:10).

We must be so united (so clothed) in Christ that we imitate His life as our pattern for living, adopting His principals, obeying His commands and becoming like Him. I've long said the greatest compliment anyone could pay me is to say, *"You look like your Father."* While I may resemble my earthly father (and this would be a compliment), it is the imitation of my heavenly Father I seek. Ephesians 5:1 tells us to **"be imitators of God."** This means we should walk like Him, talk like Him and act like Him. A dear friend of mine wrote a song that I think expresses this desire. The song is entitled, *Keep Me True.*

> Keep me true, Lord Jesus, keep me true.
> With every thought, with every step I take.
> While there is life and while there's breathe in me,
> Please, keep me true, make me like you.
>
> Keep me true, Lord Jesus, keep me true.
> Here is my will, here are my ways.
> I surrender all; I give you all my days
> Please, keep me true, make me like you.
>
> Keep me true, Lord Jesus, keep me true.
> While it's today I yield to you.
> I can only be what your Spirit allows in me,
> Please, keep me true, make me like you.

(chorus)
Keep me true, I want to be like you.
I want to walk and talk like you,
I want to think the way you do,
In all my ways acknowledge you,
Keep me true. [7]

This is the song of the free—the redeemed. Our heart has to be set on things above. Our desire has to be to imitate Him. It is what being Christian, "little Christ", means. *Putting on the new self* is accomplished step by step, day by day as we surrender to the power and work of the Holy Spirit in our lives. The Holy Spirit will begin immediately to address sin and old habits in our lives that lead us to sin. He requires the re-habituating of one's life or the creating of new habits—Christ- like habits. The re-habituation process of one's life is part of the total process of sanctification. Most often it happens incrementally, day by day, habit by habit, and choice by choice. *None* of us are perfect, but it is in our *"practice"* that we press on towards perfection. Someone once said *the definition of insanity was to do the same thing the same way and expect a different outcome.* Habits are the easiest way to be wrong again! I ran across a poem that I think sums it up.

Habit with him was all the test of truth,
It must be right: I've done it since my youth! [8]

All of us know old habits are hard to die. However, we cannot continue in the old and enjoy the privilege and blessing of the new. It just won't happen.

When my twins left for college a year ago the Lord demonstrated "the habit of the old" to me through a parking dilemma at our house. Before the kids left home, parking cars was an issue at our house. At any given time there could be three to five cars on the driveway. The rule was to pull all the way up and over to allow for "parallel parking". We've done it that way for several years. When the kids left for college I found myself *still pulling up and pulling over*! I didn't have to any more, but *out of habit* I still did! So it is with other habits of our lives. We still repeat some old things from our old life but we don't have to. Through Jesus Christ we no longer *have* to do these things. He has made provision and given us the power to *not* do them. The scientific study I quoted earlier said it takes *twenty-one times* for something to become a habit. The same study supposedly showed that it only takes *four times* of not doing a habit to break it—FOUR TIMES! Breaking habits, especially bad habits, is hard. Creating new habits takes extreme consciousness at first. It also takes a commitment to change. But God's promise to you is this…

"Commit to the Lord whatever you do, and your plans *will* succeed" (Proverbs 16:3; emphasis mine).

The word commit means "to give in trust," or "to put in the hands or power of another." It is when we release our will and our ways to the Lord that the *new self* can be shaped up into our God- given design and destiny. Commitment conquers compromise. Compromise is a tool of our enemy to get us to settle for less than our destiny, or our inheritance. Lot fell prey to compromise. When the Lord rescued Lot from Sodom and Gomorrah, Lot was told to flee for his life and not look back.

As soon as they had brought them out, one of them said, "Flee for your lives! Don't look back and don't stop anywhere in the plains. Flee to the mountains or you will be swept away (Genesis19:17).

Now listen to Lot's reply.

But Lot said to them, "No, my lords, please! Your servant has found favor in your eyes, and you have shown great kindness to me in sparing my life. But I can't flee to the mountains; this disaster will overtake me, and I'll die. Look, here is a town near enough to run to, and it is small. Let me flee to it – it is very small isn't it? Then my life will be spared" (Genesis 19:17-20).

The blessing and provision of God awaited Lot on the mountain, but in his limited and fearful thinking he reasoned and ultimately compromised for less. The town he went to was named Zoar, which means "small." Lot chose to settle in the land of "small"—the land less than God had desired for him. It's the human flaw in us all. We often want the easy way out, the closest landing spot, the less required! We all have camped in Zoar! It's compromise and it steals our inheritance.

The story did not end there, however. As previously discussed, the scriptures tell us, Lot's wife looked back and she became a pillar of salt (Genesis 19:26). Lot's wife did not take the angel's command seriously and she was struck dead. Her heart was still clinging to the pleasures of her past. Jesus used Lot's wife as a warning to New Testament believers (Luke 17:32). The warning?—Looking backwards will keep us from going forward. Habits of the past can bring death in the present if we don't let go! If our hearts stay attached to the old we CANNOT experience the new. We must flee the old—quit the old. Even a glance can kill us!

Forget the former things; do not dwell on the past. See, I am doing a new thing! Now it springs up; do you not perceive it? I am making a way in the desert and streams in the wasteland (Isaiah 43:18-19).

Nobody knows your past better than God. Nobody knows your future better than God. But we cannot live in the past anymore than we can live in the future. We can only live in the present. And our reality today is that God stands ready to transform our lives into something wonderful.

For we are God's workmanship, created in Christ Jesus to do good works, for which God prepared in advance for us to do (Ephesians 2:10).

It is by the grace and work of God that the new can and will come forth. But the requirement is that each of us must flee our past – come out and be separate. Proverbs 1:7 says, **"The fear of the**

Lord is the beginning of knowledge, but fools despise wisdom and discipline." We are taught to put off our former way of life, because it's a dangerous thing not to heed the Word of the Lord. Ask Lot's wife. Compromise cannot be our choice. Commitment is the expression of love that God looks for. It is the *setting of the soul;* our mind, emotions, and will, on things above that will usher us into the new.

> *One ship drives east and another west*
> *With the selfsame winds that blow.*
> *"Tis the set of the sails and not the gales,"*
> *Which tell us the way to go.*
> *Like the winds of the sea are the ways of fate,*
> *As we voyage along through life;*
> *"Tis the set of a soul that declares its goal,*
> *And not the calm or the strife"* [9]

Our destination is determined by the *setting of our soul.* We can look back and once again become slaves of our past or we can "set our faces like flint" toward the Promised Land. If we so choose to look forward, to go forward, then know this; every hiccup, every storm, every fiery trial of life will only serve to catapult us closer towards God.

> *Tis the set of the soul that decides its goal*
> *And not the calm or the strife.*

Every believer has a spiritual compass. Where is your pointing? Egypt? Zoar? The Promised Land? Don't settle for less. Don't compromise. Flee your past and run for the high ground. Set your sails toward God and don't turn back.

Remember, "... Our fathers refused to obey Him.
Instead they rejected Him and in their hearts turned
back to Egypt" (Acts 7:39).

Chapter 8

We Fall Down – We Get Up

…Let us throw off everything that hinders and the sin that
so easily entangles and let us run the race with
perseverance (Hebrews 12:2).

At 7:00 pm on October 20, 1968, a few thousand spectators remained in the Mexico City Olympic stadium. Earlier in the afternoon, Mammaw Wold of Ethiopia had moved toward the finish line and won the grueling 26 mile marathon. As the spectators were still leaving the stadium, two hours after Wold crossed the finish line, they heard sirens and the gunning of motorcycle engines. The quiet of the evening was broken by sounds usually reserved for emergencies. Finally, through the marathon gate a man wearing the uniform of Tanzania entered the stadium. His name was John Aquari and he was the last man to finish the race. His leg was bloodied and bandaged having been injured in a fall. He painfully hobbled around the 400M track and the spectators began to applaud. Hours after the champion had been crowned; John Aquari painfully finished the race and walked off the track. Later as the media surrounded Aquari, he was asked why he did he not quit since the task was so painful and there was no chance of winning. He answered, "My country did not send me 7000 miles to begin the race… they sent me 7000 miles to finish it."[1]

As Christians, we too, are not called to just start the race, but to finish. We are to run to get "the prize." Our "prize" is eternal life.

Do you not know that in a (earthly) race all the runners compete, but (only) one receives the prize? So run (your race) that you may lay hold (of the prize) and make it yours. Now

every athlete who goes into training conducts himself temperately and restricts himself in all things. He does it to win a wreath that will soon wither, but we (do it to receive a crown of eternal blessedness) that cannot wither. Therefore, I do not run uncertainly (without definite aim.) I do not box like one beating the air and striking without an adversary. But (like a boxer) I buffet my body (handle it roughly, discipline it by hardships) and subdue it, for fear that after proclaiming to others the Gospel and things pertaining to it, I myself should become unfit (not stand the test, be unapproved and rejected as counterfeit) (1 Corinthians 9:24-27 *Amplified Bible*) .

Paul talked often about races, competition, and perseverance. He lived in a culture that thrived on being physically superior. But such earthly races have one winner and prizes that wither. Paul talked to his listening audience about another race – the race of faith. He explained that the lifelong race of faith in this world must be run with equal or surpassing perseverance, patience, and endurance. The Tanzanian runner exemplified such a standard. *Even though he fell down, he got up.*

For though a righteous man falls seven times, he rises again (Proverbs 24:16).

We fall down – we get up

The race of faith has been going on for thousands of years. A lot of people have been in the race. In the "race" of faith, every believer will encounter things that may cause them to fall at one time or another. Most have fallen down. Falling down is not the disqualifier; failing to get back up, is. Some get up quicker than others. Some believe once they go down they are out. Staying down – refusing to get back up or refusing to believe you can get back up, is the only disqualifier. You may finish dead last, but *finishing is the goal*. Those who finish receive the crown of life. It's not about running the fastest, nor is it about running with perfection, but it is about persevering—not quitting.

Not that I have already obtained this, or have already been made perfect, but I press on to take hold of that for which Christ Jesus took hold of me… But one thing I do: Forgetting what is behind and straining toward what is ahead, *I press on* toward the goal to win the prize for which God has called me heavenward in Christ Jesus (Philippians 3:12-14; emphasis mine).

Focus in on these three words, "**I press on.**" Paul did not run with perfection nor was he the "lead" dog, so to speak. We know from other scriptures, he repeatedly confessed he did things he should not do and other things he should do, he didn't do at all. But Paul was focused on the prize. His life reads like a first grade primer. See Paul run. See Paul fall. See Paul get up. It's a racing video every runner needs to watch because it speaks of a lesson every runner needs to remember— *We all fall*! (Romans 3:23) Falling is not good, but *not getting up* is even worse. You have not come this far in your Christian journey to quit. Perhaps the way has been difficult and maybe you've fallen more times than you can count – but *falling does not disqualify you.* You're only disqualified if you do not get back up and run!

Perhaps, the Christian church has some room to mature when it comes to helping believers who have fallen. We tend to shoot our wounded. If they are not shot they are often ostracized. The biggest disservice we can do for a fallen believer is not help them back up and help them assess why they fell.

Peter is a classic example of what I am talking about. He walked daily with Jesus. They were connected by the heart and yet Peter fell down big time. Jesus knew Peter was going to fall and even told Peter in advance, **"I have prayed that your faith may not fail."** Jesus knew Peter was weak. Through his denial of Jesus, his weakness would be exposed and dealt with. God allowed the fall. The fall had a redemptive purpose – the building of Peter's faith. *Our* falling always has a redemptive purpose, too. Most often it will identify *our* weakness; a weakness that must be acknowledged so that we can learn from our failure and guard against future stumbling.

"Phillip" was a respected businessman and Christian in his community. He was a company sales representative who traveled often. Phillip was also a computer whiz. His fall started innocently. She was a client who corresponded by email. One night in distress, she divulged to Phillip the plight of her marriage. He offered an "electronic" shoulder to cry on. It seemed to help. He told her he would be in her city soon and would check on her. It was only dinner. After all, she was hurting. The two connected at a level that seemed to astonish even Phillip. He reasoned that it meant nothing. Soon he was traveling to her city often. Talk became action and soon Phillip's marriage suffered a horrible blow – adultery. See Phillip run. See Phillip fall. See Phillip…. ???

"Alice" went off to college. That's where she met Hank. He was a handsome guy and she was thrilled at the thought that she had snagged him. Out of her league, she often mused. She strutted like a proud peacock every time she was with him. She would do anything for him and she did! She became pregnant. Hank did not take the news well. He didn't want a baby and didn't want a baby on his record. He convinced Alice the only way they could continue together was for her to get an abortion. Alice had been raised in the church. She had been a Young Life leader back home. She knew abortion to be wrong but… but she loved him and did not want to lose him. So she consented. Hank stayed around long enough for the bill to be paid. That was it. He left her with a shattered life and a broken heart. See Alice run. See Alice fall down. See Alice…. ???

Peter fell, Philip fell, and Alice fell. Overwhelming guilt could have kept each in the dirt, but all three actually got up. How? Truth extended a hand and each took hold. Through caring people willing to speak God's truth in love, each found forgiveness in the cleansing blood of Jesus. Each owned their sin but realized that Jesus knew their weakness and He offers the way out of their past mistakes.

Through he falls, he shall not be utterly (ultimately) cast down, for the Lord grasps his hand in support and upholds him" (Psalm 37:23-24; *Amplified*).

David knew something about falling too! He had committed adultery with Bathsheba and had even gone so far as to have her husband murdered (2 Samuel 11: 14-27). See David run. See David fall. See David get up. Later David responded by saying, **"I have been young and now am old, yet I have *not seen the righteous forsaken* or their seed begging for bread" (Psalm 37:25, emphasis mine).** In essence, David was saying God doesn't leave His own in the dirt, but extends His hand to lift them up. We may fall, but the truth— God's truth—speaks to the fallen to declare *you will not be down forever*. It agrees with other scripture.

Cast your cares on the Lord and he will sustain you. He will never let the righteous fall (Psalm 55:22).

Never? Wait, isn't that contradictory? It seems contradictory until we go to the root meaning of the word, fall. The word "fall" as used here means *"a permanent casting down"* or disqualification. It speaks of "out of the race" kind of stuff. God in His infinite love and mercy will never let the righteous fall beyond retrieval. *We fall down – yes- but we get up*. We are picked up by truth. Truth also goes by another name. Jesus said, **"I am the way, the *truth*, and the life" (John 14:6; emphasis mine).** Let's reread Psalm 37:24, inserting the expanded truth we have seen so far.

Through he falls, he shall not be utterly (or forever) cast down, the Lord (truth) grasps his hand in support and upholds him (lifts him up). (Paraphrase mine)

When we fall all we need to do is look up from whence cometh our help. Our help comes from the Lord. The Lord is a very present help in times of trouble (Psalm 46:1). God knows how to rescue the righteous (2 Peter 2:9).

Truth is always the rescuer. Jesus, our Truth is always on the scene. Truth speaks and says I have begun a good work in you, **I WILL** see it to completion (Philippians 1:6). The church must see that we were created not merely to enter the race but to finish! Sin, self, and circumstances may trip us up, but truth lifts us up. We fall down, yes – but we are able, designed, and destined to get up and finish the race!

Therefore, since we are surrounded by such a great cloud of witnesses, (previous stumblers) let us throw off everything that hinders and the sin that so easily entangles, and let us run the race marked out for us. Let us fix our eyes on Jesus the author and perfecter of our faith (Hebrews 12:1-2 emphasis mine).

Anytime you see a scripture beginning with "Therefore," you need to see what its *there for*! In this particular scripture in Hebrews, it is there because it is building on previous truths given. The chapter that preceded this verse is Hebrews 11, also known as the roll call of faith. It's a reading of the names of the saints who have raced before us. They *all* tripped and fell. Every one of them! Some fell several times. But they are included in such a list of the faithful for one reason— *they got up*. Their faith in God's ability to lift them, restore them, and make their lives count, qualified them for the distinguished Who's Who in the Bible. Each got up by the truth and knowledge that God works in the midst of our messes and turns bad into good (Romans 8:28). Each, mentioned in Hebrews 11, finished the race and it is with this knowledge that the author of Hebrews now says, "Therefore." He explains that we are surrounded by great a number of people who can testify that God does indeed pick us up when we fall down. His point?—get up and keep running! Falling does not disqualify you. But it's not just a verse of encouragement it's a *"how to"* verse — how to run more steadfast and with surer footing.

Listen again. "Let us (that's you and me) throw off everything (need I define everything?), that hinders and the sin that so easily entangles and let us run...."Get a visual here—one of a runner peeling off every encumbering thing that is impairing the run. These days, runners often wear very sleek, aerodynamic clothing, because it offers the least resistance. A runner in the natural sense does everything to greatly improve his run and chances for winning. It just makes sense. Even though we accept this as wisdom in the natural, most often we do not apply the same wisdom in the spiritual race. This scripture in Hebrews appeals to us to apply the same mentality and principals to our spiritual run of the race of faith. Just as it makes sense to get rid of hindering things naturally, it makes equal sense spiritually. The writer of Hebrews identified the hindrances *as the sin that so easily entangles*. It's what impedes our run. It's what causes us to stumble, to trip, and often, to fall. Sin is the actual fall. Every racer must be aware of the possibility of falling.

In the 2004 Olympics in Athens, a young American racer set up on the starting block. The gun went off. The racers took off, but the young American hurdler did the unthinkable. She fell on the first hurdle! Not only did she fall, but she took down the Russian racer beside her. It was a horrible scene. The Russian racer protested and demanded the race be declared null and void. The chairman of the International Olympic Committee disagreed. He said in essence every racer must be aware of the hazard and danger of the race and that falling is potentially part of the race. In other words, one must be aware that we can fall and also be aware that there are others who can potentially cause us to fall. So it is with every runner in the race of faith. We must be aware of such potential "entanglements."

The King James Version calls such entanglements "besetting sins" (or sins that beset us). *Besetting* means *habitual*. The word *beset* means "to press in on all sides, as to perplex, as to entangle and render escape difficult, or impossible."[2] Got the picture? I thought so. *Besetting sins are habitual sins (sins of habit) that constantly trip us up.* Practically speaking, it's a generally known and often disregarded area of weakness within us. The young American hurdler will undoubtedly look at the tapes over and over to see why she fell. Her perseverance, discipline, and determination will study the fall to correct the cause. As Christians, we can do no less. Our fall does NOT have to be repeated. We too, should study the fall and determine the cause.

Several years ago, I was extremely frustrated that I seemed to trip up in the same way and the same place time after time. It would grieve me and I would confess to God and repent of my sinful ways. But I couldn't seem to keep from stumbling in the same way again, hence my frustration! Through a time of really seeking the Lord about this, He showed me how and why I was habitually falling at the same place. It was because I was *habitually* repeating *some form* of the same action! You do know there are several ways to do the *same thing* don't you? I did, but it didn't register with me that this was what I was doing until the Lord brought this to my attention. I looked up the definition of my "confessed sin." There on the pages of my dictionary and concordance were all the *very similar ways* of doing the *same* act. They may go by different names, but it was all under the same heading. I further found out that by these "back door" behaviors, the enemy was gaining access to my life. The *main door* was guarded by my repentance and confession – but unknowingly to me, he was entering through *other means*— through other behaviors. If I had not **studied** my fall, I would have missed very valuable information and needed revelation that would keep me from tripping up at the same place every time. Such study, and ultimately such revelation, which leads to our confession and repentance is what ultimately closes the access door to the enemy – all doors! Such revelation given me during this time has helped me, *throw off the hindrance.* This revelation came in several relevant and significant steps that I want to share with you for practical purposes and easy remembrance. I will call it, "**How to Close the Access Door.**"

Step 1 - Look to Jesus

Let us fix our eyes on Jesus the author and perfector of our faith (Hebrews 12:2).

Until I got alone with the Lord, I did not understand my repeated falls. Jesus is the only One perfectly able to examine our lives for sin. He alone can identify repeated behaviors that trip us up and open the door for the enemy to come in and wreak havoc on us. Jesus will always speak the whole truth and nothing but the truth. He shines the light on hidden doorways, cracks and crevices where the slimiest of attitudes and behaviors gain access. He is able and willing to call it like it is. As I began to seek the Lord, I prayed this scripture.

Search me O God, and know my heart, test me and know my anxious thoughts. See if there is any offensive way in me and lead me to the way everlasting (Psalm 139:23-24).

In the Old Testament, people would come before the priest,

according to the law, and he would pronounce them clean or unclean. Cleanness had to do with obedience to God's standard and Word. As New Testament believers, Jesus is our High Priest (Hebrews 4:14) and as we present ourselves before Him, He will examine us for "uncleanness" in the faith. He is able to inspect our lives for sin, especially *besetting sin*.

The Lord does not look at the things man looks at. Man looks at the outward appearance, but the Lord looks at the heart (1 Samuel 16:7).

All of our actions, attitudes, and motives are laid bare before God. He is willing and able to inspect our lives for redemptive purposes. Remember, anything God reveals is not for condemnation, but conviction and confession. If it comes in the form of condemnation, it is not from God (Romans 8:1). Furthermore, God is able to reveal anything that is coming against us or in operation in our lives. He can reveal where and how we have opened our lives to give the enemy entrance.

Nothing in all creation is hidden from God's sight. Everything is uncovered and laid bare before the eyes of Him to whom we must give an account (Hebrews 4:13).

Practically speaking, this is accomplished in our life when we commit to spend time with God and listen for His voice. It starts by praying and *asking God to reveal* what is in operation in our lives that is causing us to habitually sin, stumble, or fall. By His Holy Spirit, God will reveal and God will identify the problem. The Holy Spirit of God is our helper. Holy Spirit in Greek is "parakletos" which means "one called along side to help." We need such help to evaluate why we stumble, why we fall. We need such help in identifying certain behaviors, attitudes, or lifestyles that have left us wide open to the enemy's influence. We need the Holy Spirit because the Holy Spirit is also known as the Spirit of Truth.

But when He, the Spirit of Truth, comes He will guide you into

all truth, He will not speak on His own; He will speak only what He hears, and He will tell you what is to come (John 16:13).

We need truth because truth is what will set us free from entanglements, missteps, misdeed and mistakes. We need someone to tell us the truth about ourselves. That's what the Holy Spirit does. We don't always look for truth, listen for truth or long for truth, but when you are *really* ready to know, unlike any one else, the Holy Spirit will tell you the whole truth and nothing but the truth! As you pray, ponder and read the word of God, the Holy Spirit will begin to make known to you what is going on. For example: I could see a pattern of sin (habitual, besetting) in my life when I did not get my way. Ugly would come out of my mouth. I'm not talking profanity, but sarcasm and curt responses. It happened almost every time. Each time I would be left with guilt and a feeling of sadness that I had once again fallen. So I asked the Lord to examine me. I did this over a period of several days. One morning as I was reading my daily devotional, the Lord revealed my problem. The devotion was on "haughtiness." My heart tightened as I read the meditation. I knew the Lord was revealing, naming, and identifying to me what was in operation – *a spirit of haughtiness*! It was the whole truth and nothing but.

Step 2 - Study out what God names to you

Even though I had a pretty good idea what haughtiness meant, it wasn't until I looked up the word in several sources that I began to understand the numerous ways it could operate in my life. I soon realized I had a very narrow understanding of a word that had a huge impact on my life. I use several sources when defining words. My 1828 Noah Webster dictionary is particularly helpful, because Mr. Webster actually used the Bible to form the bases of defining words. Definitions in this publication often include scripture references. I also use Nelson's Bible Dictionary and Strong's Concordance. These three sources give me a broader understanding of what I am seeking. There are many good sources available, just find what suits you and **use it**! I looked up haughtiness and this is

what I found.[3] To be haughty means:
1. *proud and disdainful* (scorn, passion excited by hatred, detestation, anger, contempt)
2. *having a high opinion of one's self with some contempt for others* (contempt is the act of despising; this word is one of the strongest expressions of a mean opinion)
3. *lofty and arrogant* (giving one's self an undue degree of importance)
4. *supercilious* (I had no idea what this meant! "Super" means above and "cilia" means hair, actually eyebrows. The word picture is of someone raising their eyebrows. It also means lofty with pride, dictatorial, over bearing, having an air of contempt)

Busted! That last one did me in. I was definitely being dictatorial (or at least trying!) and overbearing in my behavior. The access door had just been identified. Anytime I find myself tempted to be dictatorial and overbearing, I can now know it is the enemy's way of trying to get into my life. These behaviors usher in a *spirit of haughtiness* that steals my witness and cause me to act un-Christ like. After the access door is identified and defined, I seek to find scriptures that relate to some form of the behavior identified. For example, I found Proverbs 16:18 which says, **"Pride goes before destruction and a *haughty* spirit before a fall" (emphasis mine).** Hello! Haughtiness *will cause you to fall.* The root of my problem identified! The verses that followed this scripture I thought were equally important and I recorded them too!

Better to be lowly (humble) in spirit and among the oppressed (meek and poor) than to share in the plunder with the proud. Whoever gives heed to instruction (God's word) prospers and blessed is he who trusts in the Lord (Proverbs 16:19-20, elaboration mine).

I sensed this would be insightful for correcting the fall. The Lord, by His word, was identifying the cause of the fall and rebuking and correcting me all at the same time. I felt grieved and relieved all at the same time. It was at this point He showed me Step 3.

Step 3 - Declare War

When God has identified what is coming against you and perhaps what you have been participating with, it is time to declare war! To declare means "to make clear or plain, to manifest, to make known, and to proclaim." This step is the *proactive step of the believer*, and our first action of war is confession. That's right, confession. Remember...

For though we live in this world, we do not wage war as the world does. The weapons we fight with are not weapons of the world. On the contrary, they have divine power to demolish strongholds (2 Corinthians 10:3-4).

It has long been said that confession is good for the soul. It is true. It is our first stance of defense against that which is coming against us. Confession is not telling God what we did. He already knows. *Confession is* simply *agreeing with God* that our acts were wrong. They were unrighteous. For believers, righteousness is like a wall of protection around us. When we sin we "bust through this wall," so to speak, and we go outside God's will and protection. On the "outside" we get hurt and wounded in ways God never intended. We become exposed to the enemy in a way that makes us vulnerable. We become "enemy bait." In the Old Testament entire cities would have a wall completely surrounding it. It was an established boundary all could see. The city was only as secure as the walls around it. The people inside knew it and the enemy on the outside knew it, too! God likes walls that are good. He shows us that anything of value should be protected. God demanded walls in every dwelling place He chose to grace. Even the tabernacle in the wilderness had portable walls to establish boundaries. Well, we are God's dwelling place today and He still demands walls. Our walls are established boundaries identified in His Word; they are biblical codes of conduct, authority lines, and behavioral borders. This truth was made clear to me in the book of Nehemiah.

As the story goes, Nehemiah had been allowed to return to his beloved Jerusalem after being in captivity in Babylon for many years. Upon return, Nehemiah found Jerusalem nearly destroyed. As Nehemiah observed the city he lamented that her walls were broken down and her gates had been burned. He cried and wept before the Lord. He poured his heart out to God on behalf of the city and the people therein. In the midst of his passionate prayer, Nehemiah confessed that Israel had sinned and she had acted wickedly towards God (Nehemiah 1:7). She had not obeyed God's commands, decrees, and law (Verse 7b). She was unfaithful to God (Verse 8). Such behavior had broken the wall of God's protection and given the enemy carte blanche access. The enemy could easily come and go and wreak havoc on the lives of God's people. Their behavior had opened a "doorway," a "gap," and caused a "breach" in the wall. At the time of Nehemiah's observance, many Israelites had been carried off in captivity to enemy country. Sound familiar? But the story did not end with mere observance. Nehemiah was determined to repair the wall and to fortify Jerusalem once again. The steps he took were valuable lessons and tools for us all. *First he prayed.*

When I heard these things I sat down and wept. For some days I mourned and fasted and prayed (Nehemiah 1:4).

Our sins *should* grieve us. They grieve God. Extreme times called for extreme measures. Not only did Nehemiah pray, but he also fasted. Sometimes such a combination of prayer and fasting is needed. Such was the case Jesus explained to his disciples, **"But** *this kind* **does not go out except by prayer and fasting"** **(Matthew 17:21 *Amplified* Bible; emphasis mine).**

If fasting is not or has not been part of your spiritual discipline, you may want to consider it. Fasting has a spiritual power and authority in the life of a believer, every bit like confession and prayer. If this discipline is unfamiliar to you or you just need to know more about it, I highly recommend reading *Fasting for Spiritual Breakthrough* by Elmer Townsend. [4] True and purely motivated fasting, has the power to break yokes of bondage and free the captive (Isaiah 58:6). Nehemiah's fasting and prayer gave way to confession. Prayer and fasting focuses us on God and restores us to clear thinking. Clear thinking, as a result of focusing on God, helps us to be able to call right, right and wrong, wrong. Confession will flow out us when we submit to such practices.

Confession also leads to repentance. One of my favorite scriptures is Jonah 3:1, **"Then the word of the Lord came to Jonah a second time**." We serve a God of second chances! Jonah had disobeyed God, run from God, and refused to do what the Lord asked him. But the Lord came to him a *second time* and repeated His will to Jonah. Jonah's first choice of disobedience caused him and those around him great distress. As Jonah lay on the beach having been vomited up by a great fish, the Lord chose that moment to speak once again to Jonah. It wasn't a different word, it was the same word. This time Jonah obeyed. He literally *turned around* and went the way of the Lord. It is a visual picture of *repentance.* If we have agreed with God about our sins that have taken us away from Him in a very wrong direction, in un-Christ like behavior or attitude, then our confession of such should be our stop and turn point. That's what "*repent*" means. It means to "to turn around."

Repentance is the decision of the believer to turn from sin and back to God. There is an enabling grace given for those who choose to turn. Repentance is the walk back into the will of God. It is to come back inside His boundaries and protection. True repentance is a "godly sorrow" for sin.[5] True repentance leads to a fundamental change in a person's relationship with God. Psalm 51 is David's prayer of repentance. He expressed true sorrow for his actions and sought forgiveness and restoration. David declared that the real sacrifice God desires is a broken and contrite (remorseful) heart (Psalm 51:7). God is able to restore and change such a heart. The Bible declares, **"If God is for us, then who can be against us?" (Romans 8:31).** Getting back on God's side of the wall is always our first act of war on our enemy!

That day when I studied out my sin of haughtiness, the knowledge of what I had done brought a conviction that led to confession. I bowed my head and my heart and agreed with God (confessed) that through such behavior, I had come outside His wall of protection and I had indeed cooperated and opened my life up to such an evil spirit. It was through such realization that brought the *grief* that I had acted in such a way. It was through such revelation that brought the *relief* that I could turn back and go inside the boundaries of God's will for my life. Confession and repentance that leads to obedience seal up the breach in the wall, the access door of the enemy.

Step 4 - Dress for War

Once you've *declared war* through confession and repentance the enemy is ready for a good fight. He is always convinced he is able to take you. He is tenacious and persistent and will not give up just because you repented. You do know there will be more battles, more onslaughts, against you don't you? God has never left us helpless, hopeless or hamstrung in front of our enemy. He provides every believer with an arsenal of weapons powerful and well able to take out such an evil opposition to our soul. Our weapons are not of the traditional variety. The everyday weapons of the world such as human intellect, ingenuity, talents, wealth, personality, propaganda, or charisma are inadequate to deliver us from Satan's powerful grasp. Such a grasp in Christendom is known as a *"stronghold."* A "stronghold," biblically speaking, is an area of our life where Satan has strong influence over us. In other words, it's where he has a good grasp (a strong hold) on an area of our life. These are areas of our lives where we have succumbed to the enemy's influence and participated with his evil schemes. It's recognizable to Christians by where we struggle in obedience or Christ likeness. We often see such strongholds manifest into alcoholism, profane language, raging tempers, perverse sexual behavior, promiscuity, lying, gossiping, slandering and the list is long (see Chapter 4). The only weapons capable of being used against these evil powers are the one's God gives to us. He knows what works against Satan. Many Christians have tried to break such strongholds by worldly conventional methods. While they may get some temporary relief they will not get the victory. Symptoms may even disappear, but the root is still in place. God's weapons take evil out by the root, so as to cut off the growth of a pervading evil. These weapons, the combat equipment of every Christian soldier, are found in Ephesians 6:11-18. Let's check our arsenal.

Put on the full armor of God so that you can take your stand against the devil's schemes. For our struggle is not against flesh and blood, but against the rulers, against the authorities, against the powers of this dark world and against spiritual forces of evil in the heavenly realm. Therefore put on the full armor of God, so that when the day of evil comes you may be able to stand your ground, and after you've done everything, to stand. Stand firm then, with the belt of truth buckled around your waist, with the breastplate of righteousness in place, and with your feet fitted with the readiness that comes from the Gospel of peace. In addition to all this, take up the shield of faith, with which you can extinguish all the flaming arrows of the evil one. Take the helmet of salvation and the sword of the spirit which is the word of God and pray in the spirit on all occasion with all kinds of prayers and requests (Ephesians 6:11-18).

Let's read it out of one other translation.

God is strong, and He wants you strong. So take everything the Master has set out for you, well-made weapons of the best materials. And put them to use so you will be able to stand up to everything the Devil throws your way. This is no afternoon athletic contest that we'll walk away from and forget about in a couple of hours. This is for keeps, a life or death, fight to the finish against the Devil and all his angels. Be prepared. *You're up against far more than you can handle on your own*. Take all the help you can get, every weapon God has issued, so that when it's all over but the shouting you'll still be on your feet. Truth, righteousness, peace, faith and salvation are more than words. *Learn how to apply them*. You'll need them throughout your life. God's word is an *indispensable weapon*. In the same way prayer is essential in this ongoing warfare. Pray hard and long. Pray for your brothers and sisters. Keep your eyes open. Keep each others spirits up so that no one falls behind or drops

out! (Ephesians 6:10-18 *The Message*; emphasis mine).

Let's be clear, our weapons include truth, righteousness, peace, faith, salvation, the Word of God, and prayer. Let's also be clear that:
> our enemy has a scheme against us
> God gives believers strategies against Satan's schemes
> our enemy is not flesh and blood, but spirit (evil spirit!)
> we are not to fight naked (unprotected)
> our protection is God's armor
> the armor is not a physical uniform, but a spiritual one
> such armor is a godly lifestyle which becomes our protection

The armor of God as listed here in Ephesians is not just a prayer, but *a lifestyle* we live. Truth, righteousness, peace, faith, salvation, the Word of God, and prayer are all superior divine weapons to fight our enemy. In Old Testament days, a soldier highly regarded his armor and made sure each piece was properly in place. These soldiers would never consider going into battle without their breastplate or sword or any other piece missing. Every piece was essential and had purpose. So it is with the Christian's armor. Every piece is essential in our protection and defense against rulers, principalities and powers of evil. *Every piece has a purpose* from our head to our toes!

Helmet of Salvation

Our *helmet of salvation* is one, of the most essential pieces, of our armor. Traditionally, helmets protect the head from physical blows. Since the head is the most vulnerable part of the body, it was the first area covered by armor. The enemy always goes for the area of vulnerability. Our head is associated with our mind. Our mind is Satan's favorite battleground. The knowledge of our salvation in Jesus Christ becomes our most important protection from the enemy. *Salvation* literally means *"safe deliverance."* It translates "to bring safely through" or "to keep from harm." Even if you lose a battle, you win the war because of salvation. Our salvation is the assurance that Satan is ultimately and eternally defeated. This is a believer's assurance:

Salvation is found in no one else; for there is no other name under heaven given to men by which we must be saved (Acts 5:12).

Salvation is safe deliverance from the enemy yesterday, today, and forever!

Breastplate of Righteousness

The breastplate of righteousness has significant importance, too. Breastplates protect the heart – the vital organ of life. If the breastplate was missing or improperly worn, the heart of the soldier would be exposed and again he would become vulnerable to injury and even death. Righteousness acts as the breastplate, the protector of a believer's heart. Righteousness is defined as holy and upright living in accordance to God's standard. [6] The word righteousness comes from a root word that means "straightness." It refers to living in such a way so that we conform to an authoritative standard. Righteousness is a moral concept. Man's righteousness is defined in terms of God's righteousness. In the Old Testament, the term righteousness is used to define man's relationship with God (Psalm 58:6; Jeremiah 9:24) and with other people (Jeremiah 22:3). Righteousness or right actions are actions that promote peace and well being in the life of the believer. Man cannot be righteous in the sight of God on his own merits. Therefore, man must have righteousness imputed, or transferred, to him. It is done through Jesus Christ. Through the belief and confession of Jesus Christ as Lord, God credits, or deposits the righteousness of Christ, to those who trust in Him (Romans 4:3-22; Galatians 3:6; Philippians 3:9). Only then does God see us as righteous, because of our identification with His Son. Such righteousness then becomes a protection to the heart of the believer.

When a man's ways are pleasing (righteous) to the Lord, he

makes even his enemies live at peace with him (Proverbs 16:7 emphasis mine).

Belt of Truth

A soldier's gear also includes a belt. This belt is not quite the same as our modern day belts. This belt typically was a wide piece of metal that protected the warrior's lower trunk and stomach. It was sometimes called a girdle. The warrior's belt was a treasured piece of the armor and was on occasion given to another as a sign of loyalty or as a reward (1 Samuel 18:4 and 11). [7] The Christian's belt is truth. *Truth* is a moral and personal quality of God. Scripture states that God is the God of truth. (Deuteronomy 32:34, Isaiah 65:16) His works are done in righteousness and *truth* (Psalm 96:13). His law is *truth* (Psalm 119:142), and the entirety of His word is *truth* (Psalm 119:160). God cannot lie, for only *truth* is found in Him. Jesus, the Word of God that became alive, is also *truth* (John 14:6). His spirit is the S*pirit of truth* (John 14:27, 15:26, and 16:13). When we align ourselves with *His truth* it becomes a protecting reality against our enemy, the Father of lies. (John 8:9) Lies are one of Satan's favorite weapons against believers. However, truth *always* dispels (drives off) lies. Truth is a powerful weapon in the life of every believer.

Peace

Satan is forever trying to steal our peace. Such a coup would leave us fretful, anxious, worried or paranoid. Such attitudes or behaviors are often evidences of "stolen" peace. The peace that protects and is part of the believer's armor is not the same peace the world speaks about or seeks. Worldly peace comes in forms of financial health, job status, and community status, just to name a few. But the peace that protects is an inner peace; an inner soundness of mind that comes from knowing that God is large and in charge. Such peace is obtained through obedience (Leviticus. 26:3). Such peace is lost through disobedience and doubt. When we lose our peace, it is usually stolen through lies, deceptions, and sinful acts. Our stolen peace is often realized by our guilty conscience. But when peace (*shalom* in Hebrew) is in place, it acts like shoes to the feet of the believers. Shoes (or military boots) provided solid footing and steadfast travel for the soldier. It is such a peace that protects our steps and becomes our steadiness as we walk through the storms of life. It was such peace Jesus offered His disciples when He rebuked the wind and the waves (Mark 4:39). It was such peace Jesus offered His disciples as He came to them walking on the water (Matthew 14:25-33). Such peace that protects our inner soul, can only come from Jesus (John 16:33). Such peace indeed becomes supernatural shoes of Good News that enables us to walk above our circumstances. Such peace comes from a trust and focus on God.

You will guard him and keep him in perfect and constant peace whose mine (both its inclination and its character) is stayed on You, because he commits himself to You, leans on You, and hopes confidently in You (Isaiah 26:3 *Amplified Bible*).

Peace is a powerful weapon!

Shield of faith

Every believer is issued a shield of faith. The Old Testament warrior's shield was a hard object, generally made of metal, with which the warrior protected the front of his body from the weapons of the enemy (the warrior had to *face* his enemy). Shields came in all shapes and sizes. For believers, our faith in God functions as our shield. Our shield may be small or large depending upon our faith. Faith is built within the believer by hearing the word of God (Romans 10:17). Faith in God is the spiritual belief that **"He is able to do immeasurably more than we could think or ask"** (Ephesians 3:20). Faith is like the pebble in David's sling. It takes down the giant! *By faith*, Noah built the ark, when it had never rained; *by faith*, Abraham and Sarah had Isaac, even though they had been infertile for seventy years. *By faith*, the Israelites passed through the Red Sea; the walls of Jericho fell down; Gideon, Samson, David and Saul conquered kingdoms. *Faith is a certainty* *in God to do in us and through us what we can not do ourselves.* Without such faith, such confidence in God, it is impossible to please Him.

And without faith it is impossible to please God, because anyone who comes to Him must believe that He exists and that He rewards those who earnestly seek Him (Hebrews 11:6).

Faith in God is the believer's protection against the wiles of Satan. The shield takes the blow, and we don't, when our faith rests in God. Faith factors in God's ability and sovereignty into every circumstance. Faith says He can even if I can't. Faith dispels (deflects) doubt, a popular tool of Satan. It's part of our armor and an indispensable piece in the hand of the believer. (For more on faith reread chapter 6).

Sword of the Spirit

The "sword of the spirit" is the believer's *only offensive weapon* to be used to war against evil's power. Satan will make every effort to undermine or destroy the Christian's confidence in that sword, "which is the Word of God." He seeks to cause us to deny the power and authority of the Word as absolute trustworthiness in all it teaches.[8] To deny such delivers us into Satan's grasp. The Bible emphatically states, **"The Word of God is living and active. Sharper than any double-edge sword, it penetrates even to dividing soul and spirit, joints, and marrow; it judges the thoughts and attitudes of the heart" (Hebrews 4:12).**The Word of God is flawless. The Word of God **"will not return empty, but will accomplish the purpose for which (God) sends it" (Isaiah 55:11).** Jesus defeated the temptations of Satan in the wilderness by the Word of God. The Word of God is able to cut through the deception of Satan – a tool he uses to lure believers. Believers fight back by the Word. We must consistently say as Jesus said, "It is written," "It is written," "It is written" (Matthew 4:1-11). However, for the Word of God to be a sword it MUST be wielded, that is, *used*! We use it by reading, memorizing, meditating, and standing on its promises. Application of the Word has *cutting power* against that which comes against us, but not if we don't use it! Got it?

Prayer

The last piece of our armor is prayer. Prayer is direct communication with our "commander in chief" which is important and necessary during war times and peace. It is my opinion that we have often turned prayer into something less than what God had in mind. Through our legalism and desperation we sometimes become "like a Pharisee" with vain repetitions. We may do so out of an unfounded fear that if we don't pray the same thing everyday God won't answer. It's just not backed up in scripture. Also, we tend to make prayer a monologue from our heart to God's. We speak and expect Him just to listen. But prayer is a two way street – it's communication from us to God and from God to us. It's great when we talk to God. It's even better when God talks to us. When God talks things happen. People are healed. Hearts are mended, and so forth. The power of prayer is not in the presenting of my agenda to God but in the listening, abiding, and, yes, often waiting for *His* agenda for me. It is in the listening that we receive instruction, wise counsel, strategies, and impartations needed for warfare. It is through prayer that God confides in His warrior (Psalm 25:14). It is through prayer – *talking and listening*, that He tells us great and unsearchable things we do not know (Jeremiah 33:3). We are told in James 5:16 that **"the prayer of a righteous man is powerful and effective."** Our prayers should be grounded in faith (Mark 11:29) and belief in God (Mark 9:23). Our prayer request should be made in Jesus' name (John 14:13-14) and according to God's will (1 John 5:14). Jesus gave us the model prayer – known as the Lord's Prayer (Matthew 6:9-13). Effective and powerful prayer must also be persistent (Luke 18:1-7). To be persistent is the same as to persevere in prayer – to keep asking, keep seeking, and keep knocking (Matthew 6:33). The basis of such effective prayer is that the believer must be in the will of God.

If I had cherished sin in my heart, the Lord would not have listened (Psalm 66:11).

Prayer is a powerful part of the armor God gives to the believer. You have access to the Lord of the army! Use it.
"Satan trembles when he sees, the weakest saint upon his knees."

Spiritual warfare is a daily reality in the life of believers. Satan cannot steal our salvation but he certainly tries to steal our witness and our walk by wreaking havoc any way he can. The battle is a reality. So is our armor. Declare war, but don't fight naked!

Step 5 – Get an Accountability Partner

The next step the Lord showed me in *closing the access door,* and keeping it closed, was to get an accountability partner. An accountability partner is a person or persons to whom we become *accountable* for our actions, ("chargeable," "answerable," "responsible," "liable"). It should be someone who is sincerely walking with the Lord and is regularly in His Word. We all need people in our lives to help us assess our lives and our daily walk—people who will give wise counsel and speak the truth in love. When Nehemiah returned to his beloved Jerusalem and saw the damage to the wall, he embarked on honest evaluation of the damage and destruction. He did it with the aid of others (Nehemiah 2:12). We all need such people in our lives – "wall investigators," I call them. Before this revelation, I was a pretty private person as far as the missteps, or mistakes of myself or my family. On occasion I would share with other family members or a friend, but it was random and sporadic, and I would only share "enough" that would still keep my character in tact. I kept my chin up and a tight upper lip. When God showed me the value of an accountability partner, I prayed long and hard about whom that would be for me. My dear friend Debbie was already functioning in that role somewhat, but I was still "selective" in what I would reveal. Then I saw this scripture in a new light.

Confess your sins to one another and pray for each other so that you may be healed (James 5:16).

Confess and pray. It is a principal worth practicing and the result is *healing*. I asked Debbie about the possibility of stepping into such a role. She prayerfully considered and said, yes. I confessed to her my fear of transparency. We both traced the root cause as pride. I then confessed pride. This was our beginning point. Debbie is NOT God to me. She is wise counsel and repeatedly sends me back to God to weigh out any and all counsel. She's extravagant in her prayers and seeks the Word of God for my life. Debbie and I became mutual partners. By this I mean she asked if I would also function in this role for her. I was humbled and delighted to do so. But this may not always be the case. You may not always become your accountability partner's partner. Don't be offended. Just because you are "comfortable" with them and believe they are the one this does not mean they will necessarily reciprocate! My accountability partner and I do not meet on a regular basis, but on an "as needed" basis. I am a strong advocate of accountability.

I also believe in inner circles. Jesus had an inner circle. Though about seventy-two traveled with Him on a regular basis, twelve became His disciples. Out of the twelve only *three* became His *inner circle*. An inner circle is the "few who help examine the wall." They often function in our lives as prayer partners and encouragers. I have an inner circle of about five or six friends that I value their spiritual wisdom and faith walk. I regularly share confidential prayer concerns, and listen to their insight. We often get involved in conversations about what we are learning from God and take notes as each walks through different trials. We regularly catalog the faithfulness of God. We have learned to pray on a new level, praise with a new freedom and worship with a new passion. They "spur me on" so to speak. They influence my life in a very positive way. They are like a "Barnabas" (an encourager), like an "Aaron" (hold me up), and a "Jonathan" (a friend that sticks closer than a brother). I love these women for their friendship and their faith.

I also have two sisters who know me and love me anyway. They have history with me that no one else has. They know my strengths and weaknesses and as you might guess, have no problem sharing what they see! (To keep the record straight – I do the same!). Both are strong Christians and I depend upon their prayers and support and try to give them mine. They are there in the midst of family crisis whether they want to be or not. They are family. They have learned to walk through the valley of the shadow of death. Each has come to her mature walk in Christ through some very difficult, tried, and tested trials. I admire them both and they are a valuable part of my inner circle.

The step of accountability should not be overlooked. I've shared on several occasions this revelation and many have come back and told me that getting an accountability partner has made a huge difference in their daily walk. Webster's says *accountability* is "the state of being liable to answer for one's conduct." Our ultimate accountability is to God, but all through the Bible we see this valuable principal lived out. David had a Nathan, Timothy had a Paul, and Moses had a Jethro. We can all benefit from the wise counsel and the healing that comes from "owning our stuff" and seeking help to walk in obedience.

He who walks with the wise grows wise, but a companion of fool's suffers harm (Proverbs 1:20).

As iron sharpens iron so one man sharpens another (Proverbs 27:17).

Step 6 – Walk in the Opposite Spirit

"For the sinful nature (the flesh) desires what is contrary to the Spirit and the Spirit what is contrary to the sinful nature (the flesh) (Galatians 5:17; emphasis mine).

I think one of the most difficult things to do is correct wrong behavior. It's difficult because we obviously have a weakness, a bent, or a rebellion that got us to the behavior in the first place. Most of us would choose to do right over wrong on any given day –

but somehow find ourselves weak and repeating old habits of our old nature and we… well we "walk like an Egyptian" as the song says. The revelation of Step 6 has been life changing for me. It was a step I did not know by name until just a few years ago. The concept was familiar but too vague to impact my life, until I really heard it that day with God. The Galatians scripture above makes it clear there are *contrary* forces within our body. They are identified as flesh and spirit. *Contrary* means hostile, opposing, conflicting, and in opposition to.[9] The scripture says flesh is in opposition to the Spirit and the Spirit is in opposition to the flesh. The Lord showed me the way to gain victory over a spirit operating in my life is to walk "opposite" to what is opposing me. For example, in my case of "haughtiness" that was identified, the opposing spirit would be "humility." The reason I know this is because when I looked up all the definitions of haughtiness, most dealt with some form of pride. Haughty as stated earlier means "to be proud, lofty, arrogant, and having an air of contempt," just to name a few. One of the scriptures that I found gave me insight to the opposite spirit.

Pride goes before destruction and a haughty spirit before a fall. Better to be of a humble spirit with the meek and poor than to divide the spoil with the proud (Proverbs 16:18-19; The Amplified).

A spirit of humility will overcome a spirit of haughtiness every time. How do I know? First, the scripture identifies that humility is better than haughtiness. Humility is a work of the Holy Spirit and this promise is true.

Greater is He who is in you than he who in the world (1 John 4:4).

Another way of saying this would be…*Greater is the Spirit of Humility who is in you than the spirit of haughtiness that is against you!* It's the ole paper, rock, scissors game. Humility will take out haughtiness every time. Why?—because it's a **greater spirit**. The Holy Spirit within us is a greater than *any* evil spirit that opposes us! To gain victory over haughtiness I must walk in a manner of humility. To do so, I found out I needed a better understanding of humility so that I can walk in it. So… I looked up humility. Here's what I found. *Humility is freedom from pride and arrogance; a modest estimation of one's own worth. It is also an act of submission.* [10] Reading this really began to shine the light on how I could walk in humility as opposed to the haughtiness I had previously chosen. I began to sense that the key to walking free from such pride and arrogance and closing the door to haughtiness starts with *acts of submission.* One of my good definitions of submission is "to yield in love." Through this step I was gaining understanding of how to close the door to haughtiness and open the door to humility. I *could* argue that if I were *able* to walk in humility, I would have already been doing it. Not necessarily so. It is often our own spiritual laziness, not unable "ness" that keeps us from walking the way we should. Besides, the Bible says we have been given every thing that we need that pertains to life and godliness. We've got it. We just don't use it! We often don't put forth the continuing effort to correct our behavior. We just do the same old thing because it's easier. Remember habits? It's doing the same thing even if it's wrong. It takes effort to make the change— *conscious effort.*

His divine power has given us everything we need for life and godliness through our knowledge of him who called us by his own glory and goodness. Through these he has given us his very great and precious promises, so that through them you may participate in the divine nature and escape the corruption in the world *caused by evil desires.*

   For this reason, *make every effort* to add to your faith goodness; and to goodness, knowledge, and to knowledge, self-control; and to self-control, perseverance; to perseverance, godliness and to godliness, brotherly kindness, and to brotherly kindness, love (2 Peter 1:3-7; emphasis mine).

Every believer *has to put forth effort* to develop godly character within. Effort requires energy. It may be physical, mental, emotional and or spiritual. Believers must be actively involved in their Christian growth. We must "make every effort" to be found spotless, and blameless (2 Peter 3:14). If we want to close the access door to the enemy so that he has no entrance into our lives, we must make an effort by opposing the spirit that comes against us. *We must come against that which comes against us.* It only makes sense to come against it with something stronger, greater doesn't it? So... back to humility. How do you walk it out? — **by practice**. Yep! It's the "P" word again! You practice, practice, practice! You begin to practice humility until you have it! After much pondering, meditating, and revelation, I really began to understand, **"His grace is sufficient for my weakness (2 Corinthians 12:9)**. His grace has been long suffering with me as I have sought to implement the tenets of humility into my life. Before I actually possess the character of humility, I'm going to act like I have it until I do! I can do so by *acts of submission* which was one of the definitions of humility. With the Holy Spirit as my reminder – every time I seek to respond in haughtiness I have a choice right then to make the effort to walk in the opposite spirit. I can esteem others higher than myself – putting them or their opinions first. I can surrender my way to follow their way. It's called "yielding in love." My practice will not be perfect at first, but the more I practice, the better I will get. On occasion I've even watched others who I knew were walking in the spirit of humility. I somewhat mimicked their actions until they became my own. *Practice humility until you have it.* It's okay – try it! When you sincerely walk in the opposite spirit, it will overcome the flesh. They are contrary – at opposite ends. This principal is woven throughout the Gospel. Jesus taught us how to respond in the opposite spirit – when He said,

If someone strikes you on the right cheek, turn to him the other also (Matthew 5:39).

Opposing what our human nature wants to do, "stuns" the enemy. He works through our selfishness, and when we refuse to cooperate, and respond with acts of kindness and humility, etc., he has no avenue to work through.

And if someone wants to sue you and take your tunic, let him have your cloak as well (Matthew 5:40).

It takes the "fight" out of the situation. It diffuses the enemy.

If someone forces you to go one mile, go with him two miles (Matthew 5:41).

An unexpected response? I'd say so. Can you imagine what the enemy is thinking on that second mile? Jesus said,

"Love your enemy and pray for those who persecute you" (Matthew 5:44).

The world says get even. That's walking in "like spirit," not opposite. Walking in the opposite spirit diffuses, defeats, and disarms the enemy. Walking in the opposite spirit strengthens our spiritual muscles and weakens the fleshy ones that cause us trouble and upheaval. You may not do it perfectly, *but do it*. Walking in the opposite spirit comes against that which comes against you. Only when such *spirits in operation* are identified and made known to us through seeking the Lord, can we combat them properly. A spirit of humility takes out pride. A spirit of benevolence takes out envy. A spirit of praise takes out despair. A spirit of gratefulness takes out greed and the list goes on. For every evil spirit that comes against us and seeks operation within us, we have a greater and opposing spirit to counterattack. *Walk in the opposite spirit*. It is in the practice of "Christ-likeness" that we will become like Christ. It's upside- down to many, right side up to God.

Step 7 – Apply Truth and Be on Guard

Just do it! What the Lord has shown me in closing the access door to the enemy is great and revelational, but it will not help me one bit until I do it! Truth – God's truth – will not set you free unless you appropriate it, utilize it, and use it. Whatever God has shown you or me only becomes powerful in our lives when we obey it. Wisdom is knowledge applied. We can truly only walk in the ways of the Lord by seeking such wisdom and understanding and then applying what we learn.

He who obeys instruction guards his life (Proverbs 19:16).

Steps one through seven not only close the access door, they are also a *guard* for our life. *Application of truth, guards our life.* We need to put that on a poster somewhere, don't we? Truth becomes the sentinel of our soul. It will sound the alarm on every opposing force. Jesus said,

Whoever lives by the truth comes into light, so that it may be seen plainly that what he has done has been done through God (John 3:21).

Evil loves darkness. Evil hates light. Truth, application of truth, comes in to our lives like light and shows us, reveals to us, what's going on. Evil gets exposed in light. Open doors are revealed by light. Bad attitudes, wrong behaviors, immoral lifestyles, and the likes, are readily seen when truth is turned on by application. The way we guard our lives is to regard truth! Many times in scripture we are told to guard or be on guard.

Watch out! Be on guard…. (Luke 12:15).

Be on guard! Be alert! (Mark 13:33).

Watch out! Be on guard against all kinds of greed (Luke 12:15).

Be self-controlled and alert. Keep a cool head. Stay alert. The devil is poised to pounce and would like nothing better than to catch you napping. Keep your guard up (1 Peter 5:8-9).

While we are rebuilding the wall of protection that we busted through there is a *continual need for guarding or to be on guard.* Never assume the enemy slumbers or gives up. He does not. He has endless energy to attack. He is driven by pride – one of the most powerful forces of evil— so be alert! Our instruction is simple, *be on guard*. Even though you have closed access doors where the enemy once came in, he will look for other entrances. He will look for a side entrance, a secret doorway, a crack, a crevice, any place he can get his foot back in to pry open your life. When Nehemiah had returned to Jerusalem to rebuild the wall around the city he encountered huge opposition in the rebuilding process. So will you! But Nehemiah made a declaration from the get go.

The God of heaven will give us success (Nehemiah 2:20).

Nehemiah was not depending on Nehemiah to rebuild the wall. Nehemiah was depending on God. And so should we. Nehemiah and his men immediately encountered mocking and ridicule. So might you. In fact, it may even come from people you consider friends or call family. Every one will not understand nor approve nor even think possible your rebuilding process. There will be naysayers! Rebuilding the wall of protection in your life may cause you to have to be separate from certain people, certain places, and or certain behaviors, etc. Not everyone will understand what or why you are doing such. Their understanding is not vital, helpful in some cases, desired in most, but vital? No. Your obedience however is. Stay the course. But listen to this part of Nehemiah's story.

But when Sanballat, Tobiah, the Arabs, the Aminonites, and the men of Ashdod heard that the repairs to Jerusalem's wall had gone ahead and that the gaps were being closed, they were angry. They all plotted together to come and fight against Jerusalem and stir up trouble against it. But we (Nehemiah and his men) prayed to our God and posted guard day and night to meet this threat (Nehemiah 4:7-9; parenthesis mine).

Expect opposition! It will come. It will be strong at times. Nehemiah's enemies banded together. Your position is *to be on guard* – spiritually alert and aware of the enemy's schemes. Remember, *we have strategies – divine strategies for taking out the enemy.*

Don't be afraid of them. Remember the Lord, who is great and awesome, and fight for your brothers, your sons and daughters, your wives, and your home (Nehemiah 4:14).

Nehemiah knew from "whence cometh his help." His help came from the Lord (Psalm 46:1, Psalm 18:1-2. Psalm 121:12) and so does yours and mine! Nehemiah applied wisdom and truth. He also posted guard. Nehemiah didn't ignore the enemy, but the enemy was not his focus, God was. Nehemiah knew God was his dread champion, strong, and mighty, able to save. Nehemiah was able because God was able. Nehemiah enlisted the help of others during the rebuilding process and subsequent attacks.

I stationed some of the people behind the lowest points of the wall at the exposed places, positioning them by families, with their swords, spears and bows (Nehemiah 4:13).

The Body of Christ – our Christian family, with sword in hand (Word of God) is a powerful force to be reckoned with. The family of God, everyday people like you and me, when enlisted, can become our "watchmen on the wall." Their job? — to protect. For Nehemiah, such people became protectors for the rebuilding of Jerusalem by watching out for approaching enemies. They were alert to any suspicious movement, any unusual sounds, and any thing they saw. They were alert and aware.

The concept of being a watchman is very biblical. The word "watchman" appears in both Old and New testaments. There are three words in the Old Testament for watchman. They were n*atsar, shamar,* and t*saphah.* All three words translate closely to mean "to guard or protect through watching over or concealing." The two New Testament words for "watching" are *gregoreous* and *agrupreo.* These words also refer to protection, but have a literal meaning of "being awake" or "sleepless." [11] Both the Old and New testament's translations paint a picture for us of a sentry, a lookout, a night watchman, who remains alert, watching for signs of trouble (Luke 21:36; 1 Corinthians 16:13; Ephesians 6:18; 1 Peter 5:8).

This concept for believers is not a physical act, but a spiritual one in nature. As has been previously stated, we have an enemy who seeks to steal, kill and destroy us. It behooves us to be on watch, on guard, for such satanic attacks. As believers, we must not be ignorant of our enemy nor his schemes to gain access to our lives to carry out his mission. We must be on guard! We must watch!

And pray in the Spirit on all occasions with all kinds of prayers and request. With this in mind, *be alert* and always keep on praying, for all the saints. (Ephesians 6:18; emphasis mine).

Go post a lookout and have him report what he sees (Isaiah 21:6).

The Message translation says, **"Keep your eyes open."** It's a must, Church! Jesus instructed His disciples to **"keep watch"** (Matthew 24:42). "Keep watch" is a present imperative, indicating a constant vigil at the present time.[12] Paul told the Thessalonians, **"Let us not be like others, who are asleep, but let us be alert and self-controlled"** (1 Thessalonians 5:6).

Every believer is called to be a watchman; to stand guard over the doorway of one's life, alert and watching for any encroachment of the enemy. It is key if we are to remain free from bondage and inside the boundaries of God. It is a spiritual truth that many of us fail to apply. Sometimes we are just happy to be free from whatever had a hold of us that we forget Satan does not give up easily. Consider the plight of this man.

When an evil spirit comes out of a man, it goes through avid places seeking rest and does not find it. Then it says, I will return to the house I left. When it arrives, it finds the house swept clean and put in order. Then goes and takes seven others spirits more wicked than itself, and they go in and live there. And the final condition of that man is worse than the first (Luke 11:24-26).

How in the world did that happen? No watchman! Satan will always come back to check and see if you closed the door and kept it closed! It is usually after our "release" that we are most haphazard about our guard. Just because you've closed the door doesn't mean he won't try the window. Your very life demands you be a watchman. One of my favorite authors and teachers is Dutch Sheets. In his book, entitled the "Watchman Prayers,"[13] he gives information in much greater detail of the role of the watchman. I highly recommend the reading.

Closing the access door to the enemy, at times, may seem impossible. But these seven steps have been tried and tested. They have helped me, not only get up when I fall, but to understand why I fell in the first place. They have been instrumental in helping me rebuild my wall of protection; get back inside the boundaries, and to become a watchman of my soul. It is for me, as it will be you, only valuable when such truths are applied. *The failure to apply truth is one of the primary reasons the church today is in bondage.* Truth will not set us free unless we walk in it. Remember when we grab hold of Truth, His hand will lift us every time!

That's how Philip got up!
That's how Alice got up!
That's how David got up!
That's how I got up!
That's how you'll get up!

We fall down. We get up. We haven't come this far to quit, let's finish the race!

Though he falls, he shall not be utterly cast down for the Lord grasps his hand in support and upholds him (Psalm 37:23-24; *Amplified Bible*)

But he said to me, "My grace is sufficient for you, for my power is made perfect in weaknesses" (2 Corinthians 12:9).

He gives strength to the weary and increases the power of the weak (Isaiah 40:29).

To him who is able to keep you from falling and to present you before His glorious presence without fault and with great joy – to the only God our savior, be glory, majesty, power and authority through Jesus Christ, our Lord, before all ages, now and forever more! Amen (Jude 24-25).

Chapter 9

The Purpose of Freedom

These people I have formed for myself; they shall declare
My praise (Isaiah: 43:21).

The Purpose of Freedom

Free at last, Free at last! Thank God Almighty, we are free at last! These powerfully demonstrative words come from an old Negro spiritual and were the words Martin Luther King, Jr., chose to close out his famous "I Have a Dream" speech in Washington, D.C., on August 28, 1963. The words elicited cheers that are still going on today. The concept of these words, however, did not begin with the old song or Martin Luther King Jr. They began with a generation of people God chose for Himself. A people liberated from bondage and brought into freedom. Such freedom evoked praise- a worship of God that brought the "church in the wilderness" to its knees.

This road out of Egypt is often long and grueling. For some of us, like the Israelites, it may take forty years to go on a five mile journey. It was a journey that could have been easier, could have been quicker, had the human heart surrendered to a loving God. The song could have been sung years earlier, but it wasn't. Why? Because the church in the wilderness did not know truth or they did not apply truth. Our plight today as the Body of Christ is no different! It has been the very reason this book has been written. The Lord made known to me that His church today is in bondage for the very same reasons as the church in the wilderness; not knowing truth (God's word, will and way) or not applying truth. The entire book to this point has been about these two revelations. God wants us to know His truth and to apply His truth. It is the only road to freedom. God wants His church to be free! Free from sin and its entanglements. But our freedom has always had a purpose. The purpose? Worship and fellowship with God. Listen again as he talked to Moses before the Exodus began.

And God said, "I will be with you. And this will be the sign to you that it is I who have sent you. *When you have brought the people out of Egypt, you will worship God on this mountain".* (Exodus 3:12; emphasis mine).

God re-emphasized this to Moses when He told him what to say to Pharaoh.

Let my people go, *so that they may worship me* in the desert (Exodus 7:16; emphasis mine).

Freedom has always been about worship. It always will be. God brought His chosen people out of bondage for the purpose of worship. We were created to worship God and bring Him pleasure. Our worship does that. Worship is the expected response of a liberated life. It comes from a heart that is grateful.

In Max Lucado's book, *It's Not About Me*, he shares a story that makes this point profound. Lucado writes,

"God has one goal: God. "I have my reputation to keep up" (Isaiah 48:11; The Message). The church, thinking with the natural mind, often acts surprised. "Isn't such an attitude, dare we ask, self-centered? Don't we deem this promotion "self-promotion"? Why does God broadcast himself? For the same reason the pilot of the lifeboat does. Think of it this way. You're floundering neck-deep in a dark, cold sea. Ship sinking. Life jacket deflating. Strength waning. Through the inky night comes the voice of a lifeboat pilot. But you cannot see him. What do you want the driver of the lifeboat to do? Be quiet? Say nothing? Stealth his way through the drowning passengers? By no means! You need volume! Amp it up buddy! In biblical jargon, you want him to show his glory. You need to hear him say, "I am here. I am strong. I have room for you. I can save you!" Drowning passengers want the pilot to reveal his preeminence.

Don't we want God to do the same? Look around. People thrash about in the seas of guilt, anger, despair. Life isn't working. We are going down fast. But God can rescue us. And only one message matters. His! We need to see God's glory.

Make no mistake. God has no ego problem. He does not reveal his glory for his good. We need to witness it for ours. We need a strong hand to pull us into a safe boat. And once aboard, what becomes our priority?

Simple. Promote God. We declare his preeminence. "Hey! Strong boat over here! Able pilot! He can pull you out!" Passengers promote the pilot. "Not to us, O Lord, not to us, but to your name give glory because of your loving kindness, because of your truth." Psalms 115:1 (New American Standard). He concludes, "The breath you took as you read that last sentence was given to you for one reason that you might for another moment, "reflect the Lord's glory"[1] (2 Corinthians 3:18 NIV).

There is only one God, the Father, who created everything and we exist for Him (1Corinthians 8:6; New Living Translation).

We've been saved and set free that we might glorify the Father— worship Him! It's our sole purpose. I have never forgotten the day the "able pilot" rescued me. My life has never been the same since. But I do sometimes forget to give Him glory, honor and worship. Sometimes I've been reluctant to do so, because I didn't feel like it, or I hesitated to do so because of *who might be looking* or *what they might think*. I've even been resistant to do so because well… because things weren't going well. My worship seemed to be circumstantial.

Max Lucado's story reminds me that I am here and have been saved to declare God's glory and to worship Him *no matter what*. I don't know about you, but I am very aware of what God (through Jesus Christ) has saved me from! If the way I was living my life before I got saved was any indication of where I was headed— well, lets just say it wasn't good.

I can tell you without one bit of embarrassment or timidity, how grateful I am that God pulled me out of the "miry clay" and "set my feet upon the rock" (Psalm 40:2). I may not say it or show it as much as I should—how grateful to God I am—but it is a *growing* gratitude inside of me. I am surrendering to the Spirit of Worship in me more each day. I do not want to ever again be guilty of with-holding my praise and worship— my gratitude and thanksgiving to God for my salvation, my deliverance.

For Christians, worship expresses reverence, awe, praise and thanksgiving to God. The English word "worship" is derived from an Old English word "worth ship," and constitutes those actions and attitudes that revere and honor the worthiness of our God, our Savior, our Deliverer, and our … "able pilot." Worship is God-centered, not man- centered. It is personal and has many styles of expression according to scripture. It is also public, incorporating the assembling of believers known as the Church. It is by God's Spirit of unity that the church can corporately, with one heart and one mouth; glorify the God and Father of our Lord Jesus Christ (Romans 15:5). [2]

Even though worship has personal expressions, it is not about style. Worship is about attitude—the attitude of one's heart. Singing, standing, raising hands or even shouting, are not signs that real worship is taking place. There *are* those who worship for show! Case in point—the Pharisees. Jesus severely chastised the Pharisees. They desired to be seen and thought highly religious. Their worship was often repetitious traditions bound up in a set of rules they had written. It engaged the mind but not the heart. Jesus' assessment? He said,

"You hypocrites! Isaiah was right when he prophesized about you! 'These people honor Me with there lips, but their hearts are far from Me. They worship Me in vain; their teachings are but rules taught by men' "(Matthew 15:7-9).

Rules for worship—ever heard of those? God has rules, but they are often a far cry from what man and his denominations have turned them into. The Pharisees had made worship about rules, strict guidelines; stand here, sit here, eat this, don't eat that. Once I was speaking at a church and the lay "leader" of the church greeted me and gave me the order of worship for the morning. I noticed a lot of asterisks beside certain songs and line items. There was one particular song they seem to sing each time I visit. I mused that they always had to sing this song the same way—sit on verse one and two, skip verse three and stand on the verse four. They sing this song the same way— choreographed and all— every single time. Tradition? Probably. Vain repetition? Maybe. All tradition in worship is not bad—unless it promotes us to be robots.

Jesus detested the Pharisees' lip service. They talked a good game, but they didn't walk it. Their faith and love for God came down to a measurement of a set of rules. Obey the rules, you're in; disobey the rules you're out. Love for God was NOT the motivation of their worship. Whoever could follow the rules best, was! They climbed the "worship ladder" accordingly. They had time-honored customs that *they* had adopted to meet the needs of their day. All of these became "traditions of the elders." For example, Pharisees were very strict about tithing and purity, so they could not eat (socialize) with a non- Pharisee, because they could not be sure the food had been properly tithed, prepared and kept ritually pure. So exclusiveness became a hallmark of the religious sect.

The main problem with the Pharisee was their attitude. The motive of their hearts was revealed by Jesus to be set on the praise of men (Matthew 6:2, 5:16, 23:5-7). They also had evil desires that their "outwardly religious" acts hid (Matt 23:25-28).[3] Perhaps this is the reason Jesus chose the word *hypocrite* when referring to them; their hearts did not match their outward appearance and God reads the heart! (1 Samuel 16:7). He is *not* a lip reader but a heart reader, and the heart of worship IS the heart! The Pharisees thought they could match God's standard by keeping all the outward rules. Luke 18:9 says they **"trusted themselves that they were righ-teous."** This can easily happen when people reduce worship and love of God to a "to do list." The only worship God accepts is the worship based on the truth and reality of who God is and who He is in our hearts. The Pharisees' worship was hindered by rules and traditions apart from God's standard. Our worship can be hindered in the same way. Our worship can also be hindered by a lifestyle of compromise, sin and immorality.

God refused to accept King Saul's worship because he disobeyed His commands (1 Samuel 15:1-23). Isaiah admonished the Israelites as a "sinful nation, a people loaded with guilt, and evil doers." At the same time they were offering worship to God and celebrating Holy Days, they were also participating in pagan festivals and rituals. Ouch! This stuck in God's craw. He said to them,

"Your New Moon festivals and your appointed feasts My soul hates. They have become a burden to Me; I am weary of bearing them. When you spread out your hands in prayer, I will hide my eyes from you; even if you offer many prayers, I will not listen" (Isaiah 1:14-15).

The people of God were living compromised lives before the Lord. They had divided hearts that were unacceptable. Their worship and praise became an abomination before Him because of the lifestyles they were living. Their hearts were not devoted to God and no amount of sacrifices on the altar could change that fact. Their "Sunday worship" was NOT acceptable, because of how they were living Monday through Saturday. God will not be mocked (Galatians 6:7). God insists we be the same man or woman on Saturday night as we are on Sunday morning. Such friendship with the world is as hatred towards God (James 4:4).

True worship does not come from an unfaithful, divided heart. King David understood this when he fell in repentance before God and prayed for clean hands and a pure heart (Psalm 24:3-4). He wanted his heart to be pure and dedicated to God and no one else. True worship is a spirit to spirit encounter with the living God. It comes from deep within. It is *"deep calling to deep,"* spiritually speaking. Worship does not come out of the intellect from just knowing about God, if comes out of the spirit and heart of man from experiencing and being in relationship with God. It occurs at a level that disengages the natural and embraces the supernatural. It's more than singing a song or repeating a creed. It's the way we live our lives. It's the awareness of God in a way that engages one's whole being and excites the soul. It's not emotionalism, it's realism— the reality of God and His presence. His presence becomes more than a promise; it becomes tangible to our senses. We are made and wired to sense and know the presence of God.(Exodus 6:7; Job 19:25; Psalm 46:10; Psalm 145:12; John 10:4,14; John 14: 17; 2 Timothy 1:12). Our worship draws on His presence (Psalm 122:3; KJV). It is in our worship that we draw near to God and He draws near to us (James 4:8). God's "nearness" will bring His presence and His peace. His glory, "the weightiness of God" will descend.

Ascribe to the Lord the glory due His name; worship the Lord in the splendor of His holiness (1Chronicles 16:25).
Praise is to His glorious name forever; may the whole Earth be filled with His glory (Psalm 72:19).

David knew about the splendor of God's holiness and the worship due God, because David was a man with a past. David had once committed adultery and murder. He, too, was a drowning passenger in the sea of humanity. But when the able pilot extended a hand, David took it. Godly sorrow and repentance of his sins followed. (see Psalm 51.) At the realization of all he had been saved from, David broke out in extravagant worship. The occasion was during the homecoming of the Ark of the Covenant. The Ark of the Covenant was a sacred chest made of wood and overlaid with gold. It had four rings of gold through which carrying poles were inserted and enabled the ark to go where the people went. Inside the ark were the two stone tablets containing the Ten Commandments. There was also a golden pot of manna that God had supernaturally supplied in the wilderness. The third item was Aaron's rod that budded to prove that Aaron was God's chosen. For the Israelites, the Ark of the Covenant symbolized *Gods presence and faithfulness.* The ark had been stolen during Israel's captivity. David had recovered it and was now bringing the "presence of God" back home. It was during the "ushering in of God's presence" that worship came up out of David like never before. Perhaps David was remembering his salvation, his deliverance at the hand of the mighty "life boat pilot." He began to worship with every fiber of his being. He danced with every muscle of his body. His gratitude was not held back nor hindered by what people would think though it could have been. You see David was *King* David –Royalty, Regal, and a Ruler. The Bible says that he laid aside his royal robe and was wearing only his linen ephod. Then…

David, wearing a linen ephod, danced before the Lord with all his might while he and the entire house of Israel brought up the ark of the Lord with shouts and the sounds of trumpet (2 Samuel 6:14-15).

But there was one who watched David's extravagant worship and was not pleased.

"As the ark of the Lord was entering the city of David, Michal, daughter of Saul (David's wife) watched from a window. And when she saw King David leaping and dancing before the Lord, she despised him in her heart (2 Samuel 6:16 parenthesis mine).

Michal did not keep her displeasure to herself. She let it be known to David. David's response?

"I will celebrate before the Lord, I will become even more undignified than this, and I will be humiliated in my own eyes" (2 Samuel 6:21b-22).

Michal thought David's behavior was beneath a King. She cared more about what the people thought and was appalled at David's public expression of gratitude to God. David didn't care what people thought. David brought his worship before the Lord. His worship was about God not man. David was dancing the dance of the redeemed. His heart was singing the song of the saved. *I'm free at last, I'm free at last. Thank God Almighty, I'm free at last!* David *knew* from whence he had been saved. Such gratitude in him evoked worship. "Worship is a voluntary act of gratitude offered by the saved to the Savior, by the healed to the Healer, by the delivered to the Deliverer." Worship is the "thank you" that refuses to be silenced.[4]

On the occasion of Jesus' triumphant entry into Jerusalem, a whole crowd of His disciples began joyfully praising and worshipping in loud voices as Jesus rode down the street. Some of the Pharisees in the crowd told Jesus to tell them to be quiet. Jesus' response? **"I tell you, if they keep quiet, the rocks will cry out!"** The glory of the Lord *shall* fill the Earth. It will come from the redeemed. Mankind, and even nature, was created to glorify God. Why? *Because He is worthy.*

That's what Mary thought the day she poured perfume on Jesus' feet. A dinner was being given in Jesus' honor at the home of Simon the leper. Lazarus, whom Jesus had raised from the dead, was there. So were Mary and Martha. While Martha was serving and Lazarus was among those reclining at the table, Mary came in and in unbridled devotion, gratitude and worship; she poured her perfume upon Jesus head and feet. It wasn't just any perfume. It was expensive. The kind reserved for burials in those days. It was a sacrificial act of worship. Mary seized the moment. The perfume poured like her heart. The fragrance was an aroma pleasing to Jesus as He accepted her act of love. But Judas one of the disciples, became indignant at what he called "a waste" (Matthew 26:8). What he called a waste, Jesus called worship. Jesus said,

"She has done a beautiful thing to me. I tell you the truth, wherever this gospel is preached throughout the world, what she has done will also be told, in memory of her" (Matthew 26:10b, 13).

The Lord ordained the story of Mary because she exemplified a heart set on dedication and devotion to him — a heart that held nothing back. A heart that was grateful. Mary, like David, like all of us, was a person with a past. Mary, like David, also had not forgotten the strong hand that pulled her from murky waters of life. Like David, Mary lived now to promote the Pilot. Her act spoke volumes to Jesus. She *worshipped* Him. Real worship happens when our spirit responds to God. Worship happens at the place where we become aware of who we were and who God is! That day Mary was so aware.

In a sermon I heard one night, Pastor Joseph Garlington

described what the scene with Jesus and Mary might have been like. It was so profound I want to share it with you.[5] He said,

"There was something in Mary that had to say thank you. Perhaps she was saying thank you for treating me like a person; for answering my questions; for raising my brother from the dead."

Perhaps the perfume was in her "hope" chest, saved for "the man." Perhaps Mary thought, but will I ever meet a man that will love me like this man!" As the story goes, Mary smeared perfume all over Jesus, (She anointed my body) and then wiped His feet with her hair. "Worship can get messy!" All she wanted to do was love Jesus, to bless Jesus. She just came to express her gratitude. She ignored the criticism and social stigma. She didn't care what people thought. She worshipped Jesus at all cost.

When Mary left Simon's house that day perhaps people looked at her and said, "Girl, what happened to your hair?" (Talk about a bad hair day!)

Pastor Garlington sidestepped for a moment and asked the large crowd gathered, *"Has your worship ever gotten messy?" Have you ever been in the car, putting your favorite Christian CD and the presence of God just fills the car? If you have, you realize in that moment the encounter and you just get messed up with Jesus. You hear him say, "I love you." You recognize His voice. You say back," I love you, too!" He counters," I love you more!" You counter, "No, I love you more." You're driving with your eyes closed (or not) and you just get lost in Jesus. You begin weeping and crying at His presence. Your makeup begins to run and you mascara is all over your face. You look like a sight! When you get to the office your co-worker takes one look at you and says, "Girl, what happened to your face?"* He continues, *"It's hard to worship without getting some on you," and there may be things that you're required to do in worship that you just can't explain to anyone else."*

"When Mary was walking away that day she too, must have wondered what had happened. There comes those moments in your life when you don't care what people say, you're going to worship! Resolve it— I'm going to worship - pour out my gratitude on Jesus. I don't care how messy it gets or who is looking, I'm going to worship!

Back at the house of Simon, Jesus leaves that room soaked with

Mary's worship. His hair is sticky with Mary's worship. Pastor Garlington elaborates, " *A few days later when Jesus is in the garden of Gethsemane, sweat and blood are running down— but is it possible, he muses, that not only sweat and blood, but some of the residue of Mary's perfume?— Mary's worship?*

Later Jesus is beaten and stripped and a crown of thorns placed on His head, His back is whipped and every time He drops his head... He smells, he inhales, Mary's worship. He struggles to the cross, they remove His garments. He's lying at the foot of His own cross when the soldiers look at the robe and one says, "Let's cut it up, lets divide it." Another soldier says, "No it's too nice, let's gamble for it." And so they roll the dice. One centurion wins and at the end of the day walking home with his prized possession he periodically stops and says, "What is that smell? Where is it coming from?" He's carrying with him the fragrant remains of Mary's extravagant worship- criticized, condemned, and costly. As he reaches his home and goes in, his wife says, "What was your day like? And he says "you can't imagine. I have no way of telling you what took place. I've never seen anything like it in my life." "What's that in your arms?" He says, "I was fortunate enough to win this man's garment." She said, "It looks expensive, can I see it?" He holds it up in the house. She said, "Honey, what are those spots on it? He said, "That's probably some of the body fluids from the beating and maybe some blood." She said, "No, those aren't blood stains I'm talking about." And she unfolds the robe in that little house and once again the house is filled with the fragrance of Mary's worship.

As Pastor Garlington concludes his story, he slowly descends to the floor of the stage and with his head bowed in his hands he began to sing, what could have been Mary's song.

"You don't know the cost of my oil, you don't know the cost of my praise, and you don't know the cost of my oil from my alabaster box."[6]

He repeated the three lines over and over and over. Soon the entire gathering of people (some 5000 people) began singing Mary's song. Some stood, others bowed. Tears flowed as the poignant and yet beautiful reminder of worship was pondered in each heart. I fell to the floor. My heart was so full, yet so broken. We (the church) often point fingers, criticize, talk, even gossip about people's expressions of worship. But the truth is:

We don't know the cost of their oil, we don't know the cost of their praise, and we don't know the cost of their oil in their alabaster box."

There ARE moments in your life when worship will cost you. It will cost you to raise your hands, raise your voice, to bow your knees and bow your heart. Some may look at your worship and say, "I don't think it takes all that!" to which you may reply, "You don't understand anything about my worship— then you, too, drop to your knees and sing,

When I think about the Lord;
How He saved me, how He raised me,
How He filled me with the Holy Ghost, how He healed me
to the uttermost.
When I think about the Lord;
How He picked me up, how He turned me around,
how He placed my feet on solid ground—
It makes me want to shout,
Hallelujah, Thank you Jesus,
Lord you are worthy of all the glory,
of all the power,
Of all the praise! [7]

Mary's worship was extravagant, sacrificial, grateful, bold, and unbridled. Not every believer is willing to worship so wildly. For several years my worship was hindered by pride—"fear of man." What would people think if I raised my hands or bowed publicly in worship? I didn't want to stand out; therefore I would NOT stand up.

I'll never forget one particular occasion I was in Memphis, Tennessee, for the purpose of hearing the Brooklyn Tabernacle Choir,- one of my favorite choirs. The songs they sang penetrated my heart and the presence of the Lord was strong. I can't tell you how it happened, but only that it happened when Damarius Carbaugh, one of the soloists was singing the song, *I Am Not Ashamed of the Gospel*. I sensed the urge to stand, and lift my hands in worship. Problem was, no one else in the entire auditorium of hundreds of people, was standing. So I resisted. But the urge would not go away. The truth was I was embarrassed to stand. We had brought several friends with us, because I wanted them to experience this choir and the worship they lead. But—what would they think? I'm a fanatic? Gone over the top? Embarrassing them? All these considerations rolled around in my head as I remained in my seat. What if I stood and no one else did? At one point I reasoned with the Holy Spirit, (Have you ever done that?) that if the choir sang the chorus *one more time* I would stand. I felt fairly comfortable in my offering because I had the choir's CD, knew how they sang the song, and knew this probably would not happen. I was safe and seated, until all of the sudden, the soloist motioned to the director to keep the song going. My heart nearly came out of my chest! I was clearly at a crossroads. What was I going to do? Was my worship about me and my reputation or was it about God and His worthiness? I took a deep breath, my heart pounding out of my chest and I stood. I closed my eyes and lifted my hands and tears began to roll down my cheeks. In my heart with repentance and gratitude, I sang to the Lord, *"I am not ashamed."* The truth was I *had* been ashamed. My worship had been about me—what made *me* comfortable. Right there in that moment I asked the Lord to please forgive me for all the times my actions had said otherwise.

About that time I felt a familiar hand in mine – my husband's. He had taken his stand beside me and soon most of the audience was standing. The glory of the Lord filled that place as one by one the worshippers stood. Later, when we returned home, I asked my husband why he stood. He said the Lord told him not to let me stand alone. God knew my fear and yet honored my faith. My fear was unfounded. It was a tactic of Satan to steal my worship of God. You do know he will do that don't you? I do. I'll never forget that day. I asked the Lord to set me free from what people think that I might worship Him in the manner *pleasing to Him*. I am not where I desire to be, but I'm headed there!

Worship is not about singing or standing even though both can be expressions and postures of worships. Worship is about God. Matt Redman (a well-known worship leader out of England), came to write a classic contemporary praise and worship song based on an experience his church went through concerning worship. In an attempt to help the church understand that worship is more than music, his pastor banned all singing in their services for a short period of time. They began to learn to worship God by intently focusing on his character and nature in their prayers and in their praise. They read the word of God aloud with new meaning and expectation. He said that hearts began to be stirred by the presence of God and expressions of worship erupted in all sorts of ways that the people had not experienced before. By the end of the time, Matt was impressed to write a song that captured what he witnessed and experienced. He titled it, *"Heart of Worship."* Part of the song says this:

> *"I'll bring you more than a song, because a song in itself is not what you have required.*
> *You search much deeper within than the ways things appear,*
> *You're looking into my heart.*
>
> *I'm coming back to the Heart of Worship*
> *And it's all about you*
> *It's all about you, Jesus.*
> *I'm sorry, Lord, for the thing I've made it*
> *When it's all about you,*
> *It's all about you, Jesus."* [8]

Perhaps a large portion of the church, me included, has limited worship to be about singing and to be about self. We often worship (sing) when we feel like it and only if we like the song. The truth is the heart of worship IS the heart. A heart that is not ashamed to humble itself in gratitude before a Mighty God – to dance the dance of the redeemed, to bow its knee, and pour out its perfume. Grateful hearts that will lift their voice in praise, and shout to the rooftops, "He is Lord!" Worship, real worship comes from the heart of man that constantly remembers the *"life boat Pilot."* The focus of worship, real worship, is God. Often worship will be costly. It will cost our "reputations," as we have to lay aside the fear of man. It will cost our positions as our feet go lower than our heads. It will cost our personal comfort as we step out to please God and not ourselves. Rick Warren, author of *"The Purpose Driven Life,"* states, *"You cannot exalt God and yourself at the same time, one must be dethroned."* [9] God is the only one worthy to sit on the throne.

When David was seeking to build an altar to the Lord in the midst of a battle, he came upon "the threshing floor of Araunah the Jebusite." Araunah offered to give King David the threshing floor for the altar site but David answered, **"I will not offer to the Lord my God sacrifices that have cost me nothing" (2 Samuel 24:24; Today's English Version).** David's message? A sacrifice that cost nothing is worth nothing. A sacrifice that cost nothing is no sacrifice at all. David understood. Mary understood. I'm getting there. How about you?

Come, let us worship and bow down. Let us kneel before the Lord our Maker (Psalm 95:6).

Shout joyfully to the Lord, all the earth. Serve the Lord with gladness; come before Him with joyful singing; know that the Lord himself is God; it is He who has made us and not we ourselves; we are His people and the sheep of His pasture. Enter His gates with thanksgiving and His courts with praise. Give thanks to Him; bless His name. For the Lord is good; His loving kindness is everlasting and His faithfulness to all generations (Psalm 100; New American Standard).

Ascribe to the Lord the glory due His name; worship the Lord in the splendor of His holiness (Psalm 29:2).

Our freedom has never been about being free. *Our freedom has always been about worship*—the worship and admiration of the One who set us free. The pilgrimage path of freedom always has the destination of the mountain of the Lord. The mountain of the Lord is the place of God's presence; the designated place where God will meet with His people. It is a place of intimate fellowship, the desire of God's heart.

When you have brought the people out of Egypt, you will worship (Me) God on this mountain (Exodus 3:12b emphasis mine).

God stands ready to bring every surrendered heart out of Egypt. He speaks to the Pharaohs of our lives and says,

"Let my people go *so that* they may worship Me (Exodus 7:16 emphasis mine).

There is a fellowship with God that only happens in worship. It does not happen anywhere else. It's the closest we can be to God this side of heaven. Freedom's purpose is worship. Worship ushers us into the presence and fellowship of God. That's why God loves our worship. It's the only thing He can't give Himself. Worship is the desire of God and the purpose of man.

I remember a morning a little over a year ago when I had just come though a particularly hard and trying time in my life. It was midmorning and no one was in the house but me. I was pouring out my gratefulness to God for the peace I was now experiencing and for the constant companionship and guidance through the fiery furnace for which I had just come. I cried tears of thankfulness as I knew the Lord had worked on my behalf and had saved me from some treacherous results of the experience. At one point, I simply fell onto the floor overcome with gratitude for what I knew He had done. It was at this point I asked God what I could to do honor Him that day. I wanted to say thank you, somehow. His answer caught me off guard. It wasn't audible, but I knew nonetheless what He said. He said, *"Dance with me."* That was his response. *"Dance with me."* It would honor God that day that I would dance with Him and so— I did! We danced and we danced and we danced. The more we danced the more I sensed God's pleasure. It seemed He was grateful that I would surrender myself to the dance. I could have had several responses:

- I could have ignored God's request and reasoned that we do not dance with God.
- I could have been embarrassed and wondered what anyone would think of me whirling and twirling in my living room with ONE you cannot see.

OR

- I could dance.

A line from a popular country-western song sums it up this way, *"I hope when you get the chance to dance, you'll dance."* [10]

And dance I did. I have danced with the Lord many times since that day. I hope I get to the point where David was when he completely abandoned himself to God's pleasure, no matter what others thought! I'm not there yet, but I'm putting all on notice – I am headed there! I do not want my praise, my worship, and my gratitude to God, restrained anymore because of what others might think or even because of what I think! I can no longer;

Sit silent

Sit on my hands

Nor sit in my seat

When it's time to honor, praise and worship

The King of Kings!

The Lord of Lords!

The Able Life Boat Pilot!

The Savior of My Life!

That day in my living room, as I danced with God, an old Anne Murray song came to me that I began to sing for Him. Perhaps you remember the song. The chorus says,

"Can I have this dance for the rest of my life?
Would you be my partner every night?
When we were together it feels so right.
Could I have this dance for the rest of my life?" [11]

David knew the dance. Mary knew the dance. Some of the Israelites finally learned the dance.

It's the dance of the redeemed.
It's the song of the saved.
It's the shout of the rescued.
It's the hope of the healed.
It's the freedom of the captive.
It's the running of the prodigal.
It's the leaping of the lame.
It's the devotion of the delivered.
It's the destination and desire of God for His people.
It's worship! And it's the very reason for which we have been set free!

These people I have formed for myself; they shall declare My praise (Isaiah 43:21).

But you (church) have come to Mount Zion, to the heavenly Jerusalem, the city of the living God. You have come to thousands upon thousands of angels in joyful assembly, to the church of the firstborn, whose names and written in heaven. You have come to God, the judge of all men, to the spirits of righteous men made perfect, to Jesus the mediator of a new covenant, and to the sprinkled blood of Abel. ...Therefore, since we are receiving a kingdom that cannot be shaken, let us be thankful, and so worship God acceptably with reverence and awe, for our 'God is a consuming fire (Hebrews 12:22-24, 28-29; parenthesis mine).

You are worthy, our Lord, and God, to receive glory, and honor and power, for You created all things, and by Your will they were created, and have their being (Revelation 4:11).

Come, let us bow down in worship, let us kneel before the Lord, our Maker; for He is our God and we are the people of His pasture, the flock under His care (Psalm 95:6-7).

*Free at last! Free at last! Thank God Almighty we are free at last!
Amen.*

**It is for freedom that Christ has set us free. Stand firm, then, and
do not let yourselves be burdened again by a yoke of slavery.
(Galatians 5:1)**

A Closing Note to the Reader

⟨ornament⟩

I once saw a painted picture that I shall never forget. It wasn't hanging in an art museum nor was it even finely framed. It was on a piece of raw canvas, hanging by a simple cord and hook at a rustic campground where I had gone for a Christian retreat. Its artist was the wife of a well known pastor in our area. The background of the canvas was painted with mottled hues of blue, green, and yellow. The picture in the foreground was simple yet poignant. It was stick people! They started at the lower right corner of the canvas and processed their way up, hand in hand to a very simplistic stick cross. Each stick man had one hand stretched up as if he were being pulled upward by the one above him. His other hand was extended down as if he himself were pulling another up. Everybody in this procession of stick people was doing the same thing! Everyone. For the three days that I was on the retreat I could not quit staring at the painting. Even now I can recall it with vividness.

The message spoke loud to me. We are all on this spiritual journey together. Some are a little further along than others, but no one gets there by themselves. We need each other! Sometimes we need a hand up. We need those people in our lives that will help us find the next step, the next level to being closer to God. We need a gentle pull, a tug, a hand, to come higher, to be more than what we currently are. We need the grip that won't let go, the prayers that won't stop the compassion and love that cares that we "come up." Sometimes we need to be the hand extending down – reaching for another who may not think they can move beyond where they are. They need us to tell them the stories of how God has worked in our lives, set us free, called us higher, equipped, and provided for our next "step." They may need our time, our attention and the truths that have enabled us to "cross the chasm" to the Promised Land.

The painting speaks of "one beggar telling another beggar where to find food." But I believe the title of the painting is larger and louder than that. I believe it's a picture of the "highway to holiness," a "voice of one calling in the desert – prepare ye the way of the Lord!" It's the road out of Egypt, the way of the cross, the spiritual route to freedom. And these sojourners are not quiet. They are "passing the peace" and telling the story that...

The way down is the way up,
That to be low is to be high,
That the broken heart is the healed heart,
That the contrite spirit is the rejoicing spirit,
That the repenting soul is the victorious soul,
That to have nothing is to possess all,
That to bear the cross is to wear the crown,
That to give is to receive,
That the valley is the place of vision." [1]

It's the story that is upside down to many – right side up to those that have ears to hear. These sojourners are God's choir to the world. They sing of His amazing grace, and declare He is the Rock of Ages. They dance the dance of David and lift up holy hands. They shout to the Lord and sing praises to His name. They are the redeemed and they so! They are not ashamed of the gospel – or the name they carry. This group knows "from whence they came," and "in whom they believe." They've been there, done that and got the t-shirt. It's imprinted with "whom the Son sets free is free indeed." This unlikely group remembers Egypt and they do not want to forget. They walk humbly before their God. This group promotes the life boat pilot. Shh, let's listen...they're singing,

Holy, Holy, Holy

Lord God Almighty
Early in the morning our song shall rise to Thee
...Only Thou art holy – there is none beside Thee
Perfect in power, in love and purity.[2]

God said, "***Let my people go so that they may worship me.***" Church, the destination of our freedom is the Mountain of worship. Our worship to God is expressed by the *way we live our lives*, by *our willingness to walk with one another*, by *honoring God with our bodies and minds*, by *our dance, our song, our shouts, and our praise.* The real purpose of our freedom is our worship. Why?— because He is worthy.

And if you are silent the rocks will cry out.[3]

Sing, stick people, sing!

"Worthy is the Lamb
Worthy is Lamb."[4]

"You are my shield, my strength my fortress, deliverer, my shelter, strong tower a very present help in time of need." [5]

"I worship you Almighty God, there is none like you. I worship you O Prince of Peace, this is what I long to do. I bring you praise, for you are my righteous. I worship you Almighty God, there is none like you. ...There is none like you."[6]

Remember "Not to Forget"

——

Get a blue tassel! Yeah, that's what I said, get a blue tassel. Hang it from your rear view mirror, your ball cap, your belt loop, wherever! But get a blue tassel. God was into blue tassels. It wasn't a symbol of graduation hanging from a mortar board but a symbol of remembrance hanging from the heart.

"The Lord said to Moses,

Speak to the Israelites and say to them: "Throughout the generations to come you are to make tassels on the corners of your garment, with a *blue cord on each tassel*. You will have these tassels to look at and *so you will remember* all the commands of the Lord, that you may obey them and not prostitute yourselves by going after the lusts of your own hearts and eyes. Then you will remember to obey all my commands and will be consecrated to your God. I am the Lord your God, *who brought you out of Egypt* to be your God. I am the Lord your God" (Numbers 15:37-41 emphasis mine).

We are a people prone to forget. Get a blue tassel and remember 'not to forget.'

A Special Thank You to My Prayer Team

Ashley Bausch
Eric Bausch
Robin Bradley
Kathy Butts
Becky Cary
Candace Clements
Carolyn Clements
Colby Clements
Jenny Clements
Terry Clements
Tim Clements
Leigh Ann Conder
Debbie Currie
Allen Egner
Paula Egner
Nicole Farley
Debbie Ferguson
Marsha Gaskill
Pam Hendericks
Brenda Hollman
Lambuth Women's Basketball Team
Linda Kelly
Rosemary Key
Chad Kingsbury
Katie Kingsbury
Jennifer Lowery
Pepper Martin
Wanna Martin
Mitzi Mathenia
Randy Mathenia
Melanie Matthews
Helen McClaren
Alicia McCoy

Brandy McCoy
Mark Myers
Elizabeth Newman
Holly Nix
Karen Osborn
Cindy Overton
Whitney Overton
Jen Palmer
Barbara Pope
Kathy Ramsey
Tiffany Shellabarger
Cindy Silvis
Emmanuel Simmons
Retha Simmons
Mike Sparks
Rexann Stanberry
Ab Taylor
Elizabeth Taylor
Don Thrasher
Teri Thrasher
Thomas Varughese
Bill Walker
James Walker
Roxanne Walker

Endnotes

Introduction

1. *The Ten Commandments*, Cecil B. DeMille, Paramount Pictures, 1956.

Chapter One

1. James Strong, *The New Strong's Exhaustive concordance of the Bible* (Nashville, TN: Thomas Nelson Publishers, 1990) 58, word #4100 Greek.

2. Donald C. Stamps, *The Full Life Study Bible: New International Version* (Grand Rapids, MI: Zondervan, 1992) 1710.

3. Ibid. text notes Exodus 5:1.

Chapter Two

1. Ibid. text notes 1 John 5:17.

2. Ibid. text notes Romans 6:1.

3. Ibid. text notes Matthew 26:28.

4. Chris Hayward, *Charisma Magazine,* "Face Your Invisible Enemies" (Lake Mary, Florida: Strang Communications Company, July 2004) 65.

5. Stamps, text notes on Matthew 3:2.

Chapter Three

1. Ibid. text notes on Romans 10:9.

2. Rosalie J. Slater, *American Dictionary of the English Language* (San Francisco, CA: G. & C. Merriam Company, 1967).

3. Stamps, text notes on 1 John 3:9.

4. Ibid. text notes on Leviticus 4:3.

5. Ibid. text notes on 1 John 2:4.

6. Ibid. text notes on James 2:17.

7. Ibid. text notes on James 2:14.

8. Ibid. page 1956.

9. Ibid. text notes on Romans 8:5-14.

10. Ibid. text notes on John 16:8.

11. Ibid. text notes on John 16:13.

12. Ibid. page 1956.

Chapter Four

1. James Strong, 95, word #6452 Hebrew.

2. Stamps, 1936

3. Ibid.

4. Ibid.

5. Ibid.

6. Ibid.

7. Stamps, 1818 #2.

8. Ibid. #3.

9. Ibid. #4.

10. Ibid. #5.

11. Ibid. #6.

12. Ibid. #7.

13. Ibid. #8.

14. Ibid. #9.

15. Ibid. #10.

16. Ibid. #11.

17. Ibid. #12.

18. Ibid. #13.

19. Ibid. #14.

20. Ibid. #15.

21. Stamps, text notes on Genesis 19:1.

22. Ibid. text notes on Luke 17:32.

23. Ibid. text notes on Genesis 19:33.

24. Ibid. text notes on Exodus 20:17.

25. Slater, "boast".

26. John. Stammis, *Trust and Obey*, 1887 (The Methodist Hymnal) 223.

Chapter Five

1. Stamps, text note on Romans 8:2.

2. Ibid. text note on Romans 8:5-14, #2.

Chapter Six

1. Heather Cooke, "Romans 8:28" poem, "Grace Growers", Graham Cooke.

2. *Karate Kid,* John G. Avildsen, Daniel LaRusso, Noriyuki Morita (Columbia Pictures, 1984).

Chapter Seven

1. Stamps, 1956.

2. Ibid. #5.

3. Tony Miller, *Charisma Magazine,* "Tune into His Voice", July 2004, 93.

4. Stamps, text notes on Matthew 15:19.

5. Ibid. 1063.

6. Charles Stanley, *In Touch Magazine*, "Early Light", August 9, 2004.

7. Debbie Currie, *Keep Me True*, (song).

8. Dr. Laurence J. Peter, *Peter's Quotations* (New York: William Morrow & Company, Inc. 1977) 147.

9. Ella Wheeler Wilcox, "'Tis the Set of the Soul" (poem).

Chapter Eight

1. Land's End Summer 1996, article insert.

2. Slater, "beset".

3. Ibid. "haughty".

4. Elmer L. Towns, *Fasting For Spiritual Breakthrough* (Ventura, CA: Regal Books, 1996).

5. Herbert Lockyer, Sr., Nelson's Illustrated Bible Dictionary (Nashville, TN: Thomas Nelson Publisher, 1986) 908.

6. Ibid. 918.

7. Ibid. 100.

8. Stamps, text notes on Ephesians 6:17.

9. Slater, "contrary"

10. Ibid. "haughty"

11. Dutch Sheets, *Watchman Prayer* (Ventura, CA: Regal Books, 2000) 29.

12. Stamps, text notes on Matthew 24:42.

13. Sheets.

Chapter Nine

1. Max Lucado, *It's Not About Me* (Brentwood, TN: Integrity Publisher, 2004) 30-31.

2. Stamps, 680.

3. Lockyer, 830.

4. Max Lucado, *God's Inspirational Promise Book* (Dallas, TX: Word Publishing, 1996) 57.

5. Joseph Garlington, "Worship", September 12, 2002, Harp & Bowl Conference, Kansas City, MO.

6. Janice Sjostran, "Alabaster Box" (Wellspring Gospel, October 1999).

7. James Huey, "When I Think About the Lord" (CFN Music, 1998).

8. Matt Redman, "Heart of Worship" (EMI Christian, 1999).

9. Rick Warren, *The Purpose Drive Life* (Grand Rapids, MI: Zondervan, 2002)105.

10. Tia Sillers and Mark D. Sanders, "I Hope You Dance" (MCA Publishing, 2000).

11. "Could I Have This Dance?" words and music by Wayland Holyfield (Bob House, 1980).

Closing Note to Reader

1. The Valley of Vision: a Collection of Puritan Prayers and Devotions.

2. Reginald Heber, "Holy, Holy, Holy" 1876.

3. Miriam Webster, "Made Me Glad" (Integrity Music).

Contact Information

Author: Lisa Clements

Address: 51 Sunnymeade Drive
             Jackson, TN   38305

Email: Lisahootie@aol.com